Intercultural Phenomenology

Bloomsbury Introductions to World Philosophies

Bloomsbury Introductions to World Philosophies delivers primers reflecting exciting new developments in the trajectory of world philosophies. Instead of privileging a single philosophical approach as the basis of comparison, the series provides a platform for diverse philosophical perspectives to accommodate the different dimensions of cross-cultural philosophizing. While introducing thinkers, texts and themes emanating from different world philosophies, each book, in an imaginative and path-breaking way, makes clear how it departs from a conventional treatment of the subject matter.

Titles in the Series:

A Practical Guide to World Philosophies, by Monika Kirloskar-Steinbach and Leah Kalmanson
Daya Krishna and Twentieth-Century Indian Philosophy, by Daniel Raveh
Māori Philosophy, by Georgina Tuari Stewart
Philosophy of Science and The Kyoto School, by Dean Anthony Brink
Tanabe Hajime and the Kyoto School, by Takeshi Morisato
African Philosophy, by Pascah Mungwini
The Zen Buddhist Philosophy of D. T. Suzuki, by Rossa Ó Muireartaigh
Sikh Philosophy, by Arvind-Pal Singh Mandair
The Philosophy of the Brahma-sūtra, by Aleksandar Uskokov
The Philosophy of the Yogasūtra, by Karen O'Brien-Kop
The Life and Thought of H. Odera Oruka, by Gail M. Presbey
Mexican Philosophy for the 21st Century, by Carlos Alberto Sánchez
Buddhist Ethics and the Bodhisattva Path, by Stephen Harris
Contextualizing Angela Davis, by Joy James

Intercultural Phenomenology

Playing with Reality

Yuko Ishihara and Steven A. Tainer

BLOOMSBURY ACADEMIC
LONDON • NEW YORK • OXFORD • NEW DELHI • SYDNEY

BLOOMSBURY ACADEMIC
Bloomsbury Publishing Plc
50 Bedford Square, London, WC1B 3DP, UK
1385 Broadway, New York, NY 10018, USA
29 Earlsfort Terrace, Dublin 2, Ireland

BLOOMSBURY, BLOOMSBURY ACADEMIC and the Diana logo are trademarks of Bloomsbury Publishing Plc

First published in Great Britain 2024

Series design by Louise Dugdale
Cover image © Andrii Shelenkov/iStock

A catalogue record for this book is available from the British Library.

A catalog record for this book is available from the Library of Congress.

ISBN: HB: 978-1-3502-9829-3
PB: 978-1-3502-9828-6
ePDF: 978-1-3502-9830-9
eBook: 978-1-3502-9831-6

Series: Bloomsbury Introductions to World Philosophies

Typeset by RefineCatch Limited, Bungay, Suffolk
Printed and bound in Great Britain

To find out more about our authors and books visit www.bloomsbury.com and sign up for our newsletters.

Contents

Figures

Series Editor Preface

The introductions we include in the World Philosophies series take a single thinker, theme or text and provide a close reading of them. What defines the series is that these are likely to be people or traditions that you have not yet encountered in your study of philosophy. By choosing to include them you broaden your understanding of ideas about the self, knowledge and the world around us. Each book presents unexplored pathways into the study of world philosophies. Instead of privileging a single philosophical approach as the basis of comparison, each book accommodates the many different dimensions of cross-cultural philosophizing. While the choice of terms used by the individual volumes may indeed carry a local inflection, they encourage critical thinking about philosophical plurality. Each book strikes a balance between locality and globality.

In *Intercultural Phenomenology: Playing with Reality* Yuko Ishihara and Steven A. Tainer invite the reader to 'play' with reality. This play, they suggest, can enable one to free oneself from the grip that one's beliefs exercise on understanding manifestations of reality to some extent. Further, that a continued cultivation of playful practice with one's beliefs, may be beneficial in exploring hitherto unprobed aspects of reality. The narrative that Ishihara and Tainer develop in making their case not only embeds first-person experiences of play into Buddhist, Confucian and Daoist notions of the same. It also offers one possible rich, thoughtful and thoroughly engaging instantiation of how an intercultural phenomenology can be understood.

Intercultural Phenomenology awaits specialist and non-specialist readers who are willing to suspend their beliefs to explore facets of reality that are manifested in experience.

Acknowledgments

Yuko Ishihara would like to thank her mentors in philosophy, Fujita Masakatsu sensei, Professor Dan Zahavi, and Professor Søren Overgaard, who have always encouraged her to practice openness in the pursuit of her interests. She has come to value this advice very much. She also thanks her colleagues that she met during her studies at Kyoto University and the Center for Subjectivity Research at the University of Copenhagen for the many stimulating conversations they had together. She would also like to express her gratitude to her parents who continue to be her role models, and her life partner, Olaf Witkowski, for being who he is: open, playful, and free. He has been a continuous source of inspiration for this book.

Steven Tainer offers immeasurable appreciation and gratitude to his wife Alicia Sarzoza-Tainer—she has, in many ways, always taught him what really matters most. He also thanks the Berkeley Buddhist Monastery for giving him the chance to continue his own practice and study, and many opportunities to share knowledge with a new generation of students. In addition, he is grateful to the Fetzer Institute and Barry Hershey for a number of grants supporting his research related to this project.

Finally, both co-authors offer their warmest thanks to Professor Piet Hut, Director of the Program in Interdisciplinary Studies at the Institute for Advanced Study, for hosting them at the Institute over a period of years to plan and work on this book. His suggestions and encouragement have been an indispensable resource to them and, no doubt, to many other scholars as well.

This work was supported by the JSPS KAKENHI Grant Number 21K12862, Grant-in-Aid for Early-Career Scientists, "Towards a 'Philosophy of Play' in the Kyoto School Tradition: A Comparative Analysis with Modern Western Philosophy of Play".

Introduction

The aim of this book is to motivate you to "play with reality." This may sound like I'm suggesting that we play around with reality in the sense of making our own versions of it. But this is not what I mean. "Playing with reality" means letting reality show itself from itself.

The problem is that most of the time we get caught up in our narrow perspectives and forget to let reality speak for itself. We firmly believe that we exist separately from other people and the things around us. We also believe that we each have a personal identity that defines who we are. *But what if these beliefs are just one way of picking out reality? What if reality has more to offer?*

In this book, I introduce the idea of "epoché," which means "suspension of judgment" in ancient Greek, as a helpful tool to open up to reality. To suspend judgment is not the same as disbelieving or even doubting whether something is true or not. Rather, it is to neither believe nor disbelieve. Or, as I like to put it, it is to loosen your grip on your beliefs. This change of attitude allows us to see more of what reality has to offer.

Opening up to reality involves a kind of playfulness and it also comes with a sense of freedom. Once we let go of trying to control and grasp reality, we naturally become more playful and eager to see what reality has to show us. We also gain a deeper sense of freedom by attuning ourselves to the rhythm of reality.

To open up to reality is to let reality play. This is why we can also speak of the "play of reality." Throughout the book, we'll be looking at the various dimensions of this play. We'll look at the play of nature and even the play of a discussion topic. We'll also speak about playing with cultural identity as well as with the appearance of things.

The main title of this book is "Intercultural Phenomenology." It is "intercultural" because it draws on ideas from the phenomenological tradition as it was developed in Europe as well as Japanese philosophy with a specific focus on the Kyoto School tradition. This means that what "phenomenology" means here is not the same as what it meant for Husserl or his successors or what academic philosophers usually understand by it today. Phenomenology for us is fundamentally an ongoing practice that is engaged, experiential, experimental, and exploratory. In this sense, it is not your typical philosophy book. It is also not an introductory textbook to phenomenology and Japanese philosophy. The scope of this book is much more focused. Its main purpose is to provide you with practical tools that can be immediately put to use in your everyday life. My hope is that after reading it, you'll find yourself practicing the epoché all the time: as you walk down your street, in your interaction with your friends, or when you're feeling down. You'll be surprised how much this simple practice can change the way you perceive reality.

For me, the epoché has always been a useful tool to engage with reality just as it is. I would say that it was a natural consequence of studying phenomenology together with Japanese philosophy that I came to interpret the epoché in this way. And practicing the epoché has definitely helped me be more open to reality, especially at times when I feel myself closing off from other people, in situations when things aren't going well, or myself when I am overwhelmed about something. The epoché shouldn't be a secret tool for phenomenologists only, but a useful tool for all of us to use in our daily life. The main motivation behind writing this book is to make this tool more accessible and ready for use.

Part 1 consists of four chapters about experimenting with the epoché, followed by a dialogue in Chapter 5 with my co-author Steven Tainer illustrating other possible forms of the epoché. Part 1 should be accessible to all readers and its chapters concentrate on ordinary life applications.

Chapter 1 is an invitation to the play of reality. It is an introduction to the idea of the epoché and what it means to play with reality. After sparking your interest, Chapter 2 attempts to motivate you to start your own exploration by giving you some examples from my own experience where I fell into the play of reality. Then, before we try out some exercises on the epoché in Chapter 4 where you will have an opportunity to explore various dimensions of the play of reality, in Chapter 3 you will find some basic philosophical background to the ideas presented in this book. The Chapter 5 dialogue with Steven compares the epoché in phenomenology with very simple versions of Buddhist, Daoist, and Confucian practices, offering examples of how you can customize your own approach along various lines.

Part 2 consists of Chapters 6 through 8. These provide more grounding in the theory, history, and cultural background of the epoché as presented here, further supporting my notion of "playing with reality." It involves a series of discussions with Steven, plus a concluding section by me in Chapter 8 on specifically Japanese contributions to the practice. This portion of the book could be read and put to use by anyone interested in a deeper understanding of the basic points outlined in Part 1. It may also be helpful for students at the undergraduate college level seeking to place our comments in the context of a more standard academic treatment of phenomenology and philosophy.

Chapter 6 discusses European philosophical movements contributing to the introduction of the phenomenological epoché by Edmund Husserl, and theoretical issues bearing on how both I and Asian contemplative traditions depart from European thought. Chapter 7 concentrates on the personal and practice-oriented side of applying the epoché. Chapter 8 brings out my own phenomenological position in relation to Husserl's views and those of several Japanese philosophers (Nishida Kitarō, Nishitani Keiji, and Ueda Shizuteru), plus the Zen teacher Dōgen Zenji and the famous poet Matsuo Bashō. It concludes with my attempted gloss on Ueda's very rich commentary on the Ten Oxherding Pictures from the Zen Buddhist tradition.

The book's development emerged from a series of conversations with Steven over several years, mostly during periods when our visits to the Institute for Advanced Study in Princeton coincided, and initial chats with Professor Piet Hut there. We'd like to offer special thanks to Piet for providing us with access to the Institute's wonderfully supportive and stimulating environment.

During our discussions, we were all surprised and pleased to find that my specific take on the epoché, emphasizing practice and re-engagement, resonates with some aspects of the Asian contemplative traditions. In fact, this connection is not quite so surprising given that Nishida Kitarō (the founder of the Kyoto School tradition) was heavily influenced by Zen Buddhism.

Overall, what emerged in the various dialogue chapters is that my version of the epoché finds common ground not only with Zen but with other contemplative traditions and cultures as well. We also explored some points where they diverge and what the implications of that might be for people living and working in the twenty-first century. Taken as a whole, we hope this book will open up further avenues for you to explore throughout the entire course of your life.

Part One

1

An Invitation to Play with Reality

How My Friend Started Playing

Many years ago, my friend had just started living with her partner. She is a very gentle and caring person and so is her partner. But it was my friend's first time to live with anybody else besides her family, and as we know, living with another person can be quite challenging, however nice that person is. Before long, they started having many arguments. Most of the time these were about small things. One day another argument was about to erupt. He had forgotten to take out the trash. "Again!," she thought. "How many times do I have to tell him?" "Why can't he remember something so simple?"

Those angry thoughts soon formed judgments about him in general: "He's always like this." "He never listens to me." "He's so stubborn." She recalls having these usual reactions and being so frustrated with this ongoing situation. But this time, for whatever reason, something stopped her from letting these judgments guide her actions. Instead, she took a step back and asked herself: *But wait, why does he act the way he does?* For the first time, she tried to actually stand in his shoes. As she made the perspectival shift, she felt the landscape change substantially. Then, it dawned on her that all this time she thought she was trying to listen to him but instead, she was only hearing what she wanted to hear. She thought she was trying to understand him, but in reality she was only trying to get him to see things her way.

This realization changed their interactions quite drastically. She became more open to her partner and to their relationship. Every time they would disagree about something, she would first listen to his views and try to see things his way. Before, she was putting a lot of effort to make the relationship into something that would make her happy. But now, she would try to let things unfold more organically, more in line with how the relationship was actually developing. This open attitude gave him more room, and this allowed him to be more open to her views in turn.

When we take a step back and reflect on our views like my friend did, we realize that many of our beliefs have been handed down to us by the environment we grew up in. In English, you can say that someone is "seeing with rose-colored glasses" when they have an overly optimistic view of things.

In Japanese, we say "seeing with colored glasses" (*iromegane de miru*, 色眼鏡で見る) to generally refer to people's perceptions that have been filtered by biases and projections. These biases aren't necessarily wrong, but they do color our view of reality. After realizing that both she and her partner were seeing reality through their own colored glasses, my friend was able to take some distance from her initial perception. And once a space had opened up between her and her colored glasses, she could sift through to see which of her old beliefs she should keep and which she should perhaps get rid of. The nice thing about being a couple is that you can do this sifting process together.

What is the "Epoché"?

My friend's situation—where we are naturally led to become aware of our colored glasses—is not so common. When such situations arise, that's great and we can view them as occasions to learn from them. But instead of waiting for this kind of occasion to occur spontaneously, it would help a great deal if we could somehow nurture a way of being open to reality without always being caught up in our own ways of seeing reality. This is part of what the method of the "epoché" allows us to do.

Epoché in ancient Greek means *suspension of judgment*. For example, instead of believing that this book is going to be a huge hit, I suspend my judgment on its success or failure. This doesn't mean I stop believing that it will be a success in the sense that I disbelieve it. Rather, I simply refrain from making any judgment on the book with regard to its possible success or failure. I neither believe nor disbelieve. I neutralize my belief in relation to these possibilities.

But what good does this do? Why should we practice the epoché? When we believe in something, we often find ourselves getting caught up in the belief, investing much effort to believe in our belief, instead of using that same effort to check the belief against reality. My belief that the book is going to be a success may keep me from looking at it with a critical eye that could possibly improve the content of the book. Even if someone with a good heart were to offer some suggestions on how to improve it, I might be offended just because my belief says it's good enough. Often, our belief in our belief keeps us stuck in our narrow ways of looking at reality and blind to the other possible ways.

The more time and effort we invest in our beliefs (and our beliefs in our beliefs), the more difficult it is to change them. Some of our beliefs may have become so fixed throughout all these years that we may have even forgotten that they are beliefs, which may or may not be true. The arguments that my friend was having with her partner were mostly due to a clash between the habitual ways of seeing and doing things, which are just another form of fixed beliefs. Therefore, the first important step of the epoché is to acknowledge or recognize your beliefs *as beliefs*.

Once you have acknowledged their belief character, you can begin to *loosen your grip* on them. This is what we mean by "suspension of judgment." To use the expressions of the phenomenologist Edmund Husserl, we "bracket" or "put it out of play."[1] I prefer the imagery of letting your grip loosen up, since it fits nicely with that feeling of ease that comes from releasing the tightness you have when you are holding on tightly to a belief.

Loosening your grip on a belief doesn't mean you have to completely let it go. It just means you temporarily set the belief aside so that the belief doesn't color your reality anymore. This is a powerful move that allows you to be more open to reality and what it has to offer. This openness in turn allows us to "play with reality." But what does this actually mean? And how do we do it?

Taking Off Your Colored Glasses

As mentioned earlier, in Japanese we say "seeing with colored glasses" to refer to a perception of reality that has been filtered by biases and projections. So, another metaphor for the epoché is acknowledging that you have a pair of colored glasses on and then, subsequently, taking them off. Again, you don't have to get rid of them, you just need to set them aside for a moment. Although this is already an important move in itself, one that requires much diligence, this is just the start of the exciting exploration that follows.

Let's say that you have lived your whole life wearing a pair of yellow-lensed glasses. You believe that the world is in fact yellow. But then you meet a bunch of people who tell you that lemons are yellow, but limes are green. You initially think they are just wrong (you think maybe "green" is a name of a different shade of yellow…?) but then you begin to wonder if you're actually missing out on something. After much self-scrutiny, you finally realize that it is not that the world is yellow, but that your perception is coloring the world yellow. Shocked by this finding but eager to see what would happen, you slowly take your colored glasses off … What a surprise! How colorful the world is! You realize how much your colored glasses have been distorting your view of reality and how much there is to discover. You can then look at the sky all day, mesmerized by the change of colors at dawn, during the day, and at dusk. You walk around your neighborhood to explore the different colors of houses and learn something new about your neighbors' tastes. You have been liberated from your narrow perspective and have started playing with reality.

Playing with reality means you become co-players with reality. It doesn't mean that you mess around with reality by creating your own versions of it. It is quite the opposite. You let reality speak for itself, to show itself from itself, rather than you speaking for it. But this doesn't mean you just become passive and do nothing. This requires a different kind of doing on our part than what we do when we project our own understanding onto reality. You tune in to the natural rhythm of things and let things unfold according to their own way of being. In the above case, it means you tune in to the colors themselves and the way the different colors interact with each other. In the case of my friend and her partner, it might involve attuning to each other's way of being and to the natural movement of the relationship. Or you could play with reality by listening to your own mind and body and living in harmony with what is right for your well-being. In all of these cases, there is no molding of reality to make it fit your way. Instead, you are letting the true nature of reality present itself as you listen attentively to reality speaking for itself.

Where Does the Epoché Take Us?

I should note at this point that playing with reality in the above sense of becoming co-partners with reality doesn't mean that you have to completely tune in to every aspect of reality. It doesn't mean that we have to take off *all* our colored glasses. One day, you may wake up to a gloomy day outside. That might immediately make you unmotivated and depressed. But if you were to set aside the belief that the day is gloomy, you may realize that the sunless gray sky actually has its own charm and is quite beautiful as it is. This new fascination may soon clear your dark mood, inviting you to appreciate the "gloomy" weather in its own right. What the experience here shows is how much removing a single pair of colored glasses, and a rather simple one too, can already make a big difference in the way we practically engage with the world and to the others around us. This simple suspension of judgment on the gloomy weather could save you from creating a tense environment at work, and needless stress on your colleagues. Instead of complaining about the lack of sunshine and how you couldn't go running because of the bad weather, you could share your new amusement with the beautiful gray sky and spread your joy to others.

However wonderful this may be, you may say that there seems to be a large gap between doing just that and trying to remove all our colored glasses. Sure, we can all relate to our past experiences where we benefited from setting aside some of our beliefs and letting reality surprise us. But that doesn't mean we were effectively seeing reality as it is in itself, completely untainted by all our judgments. We might be exchanging an old pair of glasses with newer, more refined ones, but however much we improve, we're always seeing reality through some colored glasses. Or so you may say.

But let us pause here for a second. Why should we either believe or disbelieve that seeing reality without any colored glasses is possible? If our experiences have shown that the practice of suspending judgment has some positive practical outcome of revealing something more about reality, then perhaps we can suspend judgment about the possibility of suspending all judgments? We neither believe nor disbelieve that it is possible for us to understand reality as it is in itself. This doesn't mean we deny the possibility. But it also doesn't mean we affirm it. Practicing the epoché on this particular state of affairs allows us to have an open attitude about what it is that it ultimately attempts to achieve. Practicing the epoché doesn't have a final goal. The main idea is to play with reality which is so enjoyable in itself that, like with other sorts of play, you wouldn't want it to come to an end. The epoché is simply a tool for us to do that.

Loosening Your Grip on Perception

Let's now try a simple exercise where we try out the epoché on our perception of an object. You'll be surprised to find that something as seemingly simple as our perception of an object is already full of filters. Take any object, say a cup, that is in front of you. Looking at it, you believe that the cup is there in front of you. Now try negating that belief; entertain the belief that the cup is *not* in front of you. To help you with this, you can imagine a situation where you are in front of a very realistic painting of a cup. Or if it works better for you, imagine that you are in a virtual reality. What you are actually seeing is not a cup but a computer simulation of a cup. It looks very real, but you know that the cup is not really in front of you. These imagined situations will help you get an actual feel of having such disbelief. Once you believe in this disbelief, note the difference in the two attitudes. How does disbelieving that the cup is in front of you differ from believing?

You might find that however much you try to believe in your disbelief, you can't really convince yourself that the cup is in fact not in front of you. This just shows how much the sense of directly seeing an object together with the surrounding knowledge (like your knowledge based on your memory that you put this cup there a few minutes ago) contributes to your belief in your perception. Taking note of this tightness or closeness you feel towards your belief, try to now loosen your grip on it. Suspend your judgment and neither believe nor disbelieve that the cup is in front of you. Just as taking up the cup in your hand is a possibility, note that believing and disbelieving are also possibilities for you. And let them both *remain* possibilities for you. You may feel a bit more distanced towards the object because now you're not straightforwardly seeing it but instead are seeing it from a suspended attitude which creates a distance to your belief in the object. This kind of attitude is not natural for us so it's going to feel rather odd. But embrace the oddity of this attitude and try to stay with it for a while.

Once you feel more or less comfortable with this, try to let the cup appear to you in your experience untainted by the coloring of your judgments. Try focusing purely on the way in which "the cup" appears to you in your experience.

If you sit down with this experiment for a bit, you may soon notice that your sensation of "the cup" is constantly changing in your experience (due to the reflections of the light, depending on the angle you are seeing it from, etc.). When you make the judgment that this thing you are seeing is a cup, you effectively disregard these myriad features of your experience. You might also notice that when you say that "the cup is in front of me," you don't in fact see the whole cup but only an aspect of it. Nonetheless, you still somehow experience the whole cup. In making judgments, we are always cutting out and interpreting the appearance of things in a specific way. There is therefore a rather large gap between our judgments and the actual appearance of things.

If you stick with this experiment long enough, and really play with the appearance of things, you may even realize that one of the basic filters we use in our perception is the subject-object duality. However much you try to simply let the thing appear, you may find it difficult to put aside the basic belief that "I" am here and "the cup" is over there. But what if we set aside this dualistic framework? How do things appear now?

There will be many more things you may notice once you have deactivated your judgments. Some of these things may seem trivial while others will be quite profound, so much so that you may have to re-evaluate your beliefs. If we really want to see what we could discover from suspending judgment on our perception, it would take much more practice. Perhaps it is the first time it has occurred to you that you can set aside the subject-object duality. If you're confused, that's okay. Recognizing this as a framework will already be a big step forward. Then setting it aside will be another big challenge but quite an exciting one. We'll try some more exercises like this with more focus in Chapter 4 and we'll explore various dimensions of the epoché in more depth. But the purpose of introducing this exercise here was to give you some idea of how the suspension of judgment could be an effective method for discovering those aspects of reality that are otherwise hidden underneath our judgments. By realizing the gap between our judgments and the appearance of reality, you nurture a sense of humbleness towards your own perspective and an openness to reality.

In this chapter, we looked at two examples of how suspension of judgment could be a helpful way of opening up to reality. We saw how my friend benefited from spontaneously suspending her judgment, which allowed her to be more open to her partner. We also saw how suspending judgment on a seemingly simpler case of a perception of an object could open us up to things and the way they appear to us. This kind of openness to others and things provides us with an opportunity to discover more by tuning in to them and letting them show themselves from themselves. This way of relating to reality is what I have called "playing with reality."

A Short Note on Husserl's Version of the Epoché

Before ending this chapter, which was intended as an invitation to play with reality, I will briefly comment on the main inspiration of the version of the epoché that I am presenting in this book. This is the "phenomenological epoché" introduced by the German philosopher Edmund Husserl (1859–1938) at the beginning of the twentieth century as a core method for a new science called phenomenology. According to Husserl, most sciences that deal with reality, whether the physical, the mathematical, or the social and historical reality, uncritically believe in the existence of the world. This is the physical, social, and historical world filled with various meanings and values. While this may be a fair assumption to make for a scientist, for a philosopher interested in securing firm foundations for the sciences, this belief had to be called into question. But instead of taking up the perennial metaphysical question about the existence of the world, which doesn't get us anywhere, he found a way to stay close to our experience: he suspended judgment about the existential status of the world. By setting aside our concern about whether or not the world really exists, he could simply focus on phenomena, that is, that which present themselves to us in our experience. This effectively opened up a completely new field of study called phenomenology: a study of how things present themselves in our experience purely in the way they show themselves in themselves.

Husserl's revival of the idea of suspending judgment, which goes back to the Skeptic tradition in ancient Greece, was tremendously significant for philosophy. In Husserl's hands, the epoché became a core method for any area of study interested in understanding the way in which things appear to us in our experience from the first-person point of view.[2] But because

Husserl's interest was so specific, Husserl's version of the epoché was also quite specific. The open attitude characteristic of the epoché became more of a specific attitude for phenomenologists and less of a general attitude for us all to help with our practical lives.

We'll see more about Husserl's phenomenological epoché as well as other relevant philosophical ideas in Chapter 3. You will see how my idea of the epoché as a way to play with reality is only somewhat related to Husserl's original version. It also has roots in other phenomenological sources including the hermeneutic phenomenology of Hans-Georg Gadamer and Paul Ricoeur, as well as the Kyoto School tradition of Japanese philosophy, specifically the philosophy of Nishida Kitarō (西田幾多郎, 1870–1945). You will also learn how Japanese culture forms an important background to my interpretation of the epoché and play, which is something that will be discussed in Chapter 8. Therefore, the version of the epoché that you will find in this book will be quite different from Husserl's in various respects. Most importantly, it is different in that it doesn't purport to be a fancy method for specialists only. It is for everyone who has a sincere interest in understanding the nature of reality and our place in it. The aim of this book is to get you motivated to play with reality. The epoché is presented to serve this purpose. By practicing the epoché, we can learn to play with reality.

Discussion Questions

- A central focus of Chapter 1 is "seeing with colored glasses." Can you identify several examples of this limited way of seeing in your own life? Can you apply the epoché (suspension of judgment) to them?
- When you apply the epoché to some of your colored glasses, do you find that some are more difficult to suspend than others? Why do you think so?
- The epoché is not an end in itself but a tool to open up to reality (what we called "playing with reality"). Do you feel more open to reality after suspending judgment? If not, how do you feel?
- We raised an example of how someone may say that it is not possible to see reality without *any* colored glasses. If you feel that objection has merit, it may be worthwhile to stop and ask yourself why you feel that way. Could you try to set aside this belief just for a moment (which is not to say that you need to get rid of the belief)?

2

Falling into Play

As we saw in Chapter 1, the purpose of this book is to motivate you to play with reality in the sense of becoming co-players with reality. But we cannot become motivated about something we are not familiar with. Therefore, before we take a closer look at the ideas of the epoché and playing with reality and try out the various exercises to help you practice them, I want us to get a solid sense of what it is like to play with reality by looking into our own experiences. All of us have experienced spontaneously falling into the play of reality just like my friend did in her relationship.[1] So it is just a matter of reflecting on our experiences and identifying those occasions as an instance of playing with reality. To help you with this, I have given a few examples from my own experience where I fell into the various dimensions of this play of reality: the play of cultural reality; the play of a discussion topic; the play of the appearance of reality; and the play of nature.[2] I hope you will be able to relate to some of these examples and use them as a guide to find examples from your own experience.

Case 1: Encountering the Unfamiliar

I will start with an example from my upbringing. This is an example of how encountering the unfamiliar could enable us to become aware of some of the cultural biases we have.

I was born and brought up in a mid-sized town in Texas called Lubbock. Since my parents are Japanese and they wanted to make sure we learned to speak Japanese fluently and become acquainted with the Japanese culture, every summer we spent two months in Tokyo where I went to a local school just around the corner of my grandparents' house. Even though that meant less vacation for me, I don't recall ever complaining about that since I genuinely enjoyed having a second school life there. In fact, even though my home was physically in Lubbock, and I had many good friends there, I somehow felt more at home in Japan. I was basically the only Asian at school (except for my siblings) and even though I was never really bullied for that, I still felt that I was different just because I looked different. I felt that I didn't fit in.

That is why when my parents told me at the age of 13 that we were officially moving to Japan, I was really happy, and I even felt a sense of relief. Finally, I thought, I will feel at home. But it didn't take long to realize that this was a false hope. Spending two months a year in Japan wasn't the same as settling down and really becoming integrated there. I did look like my peers but that was about it. If you've lived in Japan for some time, you would know that there are so many tedious social norms attached to "being Japanese." There is typically one right way of responding to social situations and if you do something slightly different, you're labeled "that odd one."

My parents had heard from their friends how difficult it is for a returnee child to fit into a Japanese school, so they took precautions. Thanks to them, I was never bullied. But that also meant that I had to make a conscious effort to act like a Japanese girl. Sometimes I asked my friends why they did the things that they did, like why girls go to the bathroom together in a group(!), but I never really got a proper answer. Most of them didn't understand my question and just looked at me in an odd way. This is quite understandable since there was no good reason why they should reflect on their social norms and customs. For them, it was natural to unquestionably follow what everyone else does.

When I moved to Japan and tried to integrate into Japanese school life, I was struck by the fact that I wasn't wearing the same-colored glasses as my Japanese friends. To my surprise, I was in fact wearing American-colored glasses. In order to integrate, I had to set aside my American-colored glasses so that I could "play" with the Japanese cultural reality. Of course, back then, it wasn't such a playful thing for me. I basically had no choice but to put aside the old glasses for the new ones if I wanted to fit in. Although it wasn't always easy, I am very grateful for having had this unique childhood where I could take a detached view to my cultures in a way that is neither natural nor easy for someone who is brought up in a single culture. I didn't deliberately take a distant view, but my circumstances allowed me to become distanced from them. Put differently, I was naturally trained to recognize my culturally colored glasses *as culturally colored glasses*. Even if you weren't brought up in between cultures like I was, if you've lived abroad for some time or have close friends who are brought up in a different culture to yours, you have probably experienced something similar. Oftentimes, our encounter with the unfamiliar allows us to create a healthy distance from our own culture, making us aware of our culturally colored glasses and letting us genuinely enjoy the play of cultural reality. When did you fall into the play of cultural reality?

Case 2: Losing Yourself in a Compelling Topic

In Chapter 1, we saw the example of my friend who spontaneously dropped her narrow perspective. Although it's difficult to determine what exactly motivated her to do so, it was probably prompted by the genuine intention to understand her partner for who he is. Let us now look at an example of how a similar thing can happen when a deep interest in a topic can make you set aside your beliefs and projections.

I have been part of the academic community for around ten years now, counting back from the time when I started getting serious about pursuing a career in philosophy. And throughout those years, I have had numerous occasions to talk with my friends and colleagues about various questions in philosophy, from the more abstract metaphysical questions to the more concrete existential questions concerning the meaning of life.

But the discussions were not always so engaging. Sometimes I was just not really excited about the topic or if I was, others were not. If you're talking to someone one-on-one, it's usually not difficult to find a topic of common interest and let the conversation unfold. However, in a group this is not so easy. Even when everyone is excited about the topic, there are other obstacles that distract us from engaging in the discussion. Most notably, there are the eyes of others. As soon as we have more than one pair of eyes looking, we tend to become more self-conscious. "What would they think if I say this or that?" "What if they think I am stupid?"

Aside from these worries about others' judgments on yourself, you may feel pressured to show them that you are knowledgeable. Or you might put pressure on yourself to come up with better responses than others. Or self-doubt might creep in, making you question your own abilities. All these beliefs and projections stand in the way of really engaging with the discussion. I must say that most of the time, at least at the beginning of a discussion, I have to deal with all these side issues instead of the real issue on the table.

But gradually, as you tune into the topic, you start to lose yourself in the discussion. Oftentimes this happens on its own, when the topic is compelling enough to fully grab your attention. The center of your attention moves away from you to the topic itself. All those worries that stem from you being so self-absorbed are somehow dropped. You can even feel yourself dissolving into something larger than yourself.

When the other people also start getting immersed and the group dynamics are working well, you may even get the sense that the discussion is unfolding on its own. Nobody is in control and no strenuous effort has to be made to come up with interesting ideas. Instead, it is as if the discussion has a life of its own that is naturally developing. New and fascinating ideas spontaneously emerge, not so much out of the individuals (though surely each individual contributes their individuality), but from the dynamic movement of the discussion. And the more you tune in, listening to the way the discussion is moving, the more you can feel yourself becoming part of the dynamic play of the topic. Interestingly, this kind of thing usually happens only after long periods of deliberation and dialogue. It seems that when our understandings have deepened enough, there comes a time when the discussion just starts to play itself out, very naturally.[3]

You know that something like this was happening in an intensive manner when you can recall important ideas, but you can't remember who said them and you also feel that it's not really important. What was important is that interesting ideas emerged out of the place that gathered the people in a way that brought life to the discussion. I often realize after having these experiences how much my initial worries were getting in the way of this kind of engaged discussion. Just as my friend's genuine intention to understand her partner led to her realization, our deep interest in a topic, whatever it may be, can lead us to realize how much we are holding ourselves back from getting a better understanding of things. Perhaps you can recall an occasion or two when something like this has happened to you where you naturally let go of your projections and beliefs and enjoyed the topic playing itself out.

Case 3: Seeing More Through Art

Encountering the unfamiliar and engaging with other people, whether with our partners or in a group, are all nice examples of how we can spontaneously fall into the play of reality, where we naturally take a distance to our colored glasses. Here is another example from our daily lives with a slightly different flavor: *learning to see more through art.*

I don't regard myself as a very artsy person in general and I don't feel I have the ability to appreciate art in ways that some people do. But I remember this one occasion when a painting caught my attention so much that I couldn't move for some time. It was an oil painting of three peaches on a plate by the French painter, Henri Fantin-Latour. Compared to the other paintings in the museum, it was relatively small and probably not the most impressive. After all, it was just a painting of some peaches. But I was struck by how real they were. My mouth immediately started getting watery and I could almost smell them. They were a bit too ripe, just the way I like them.

Figure 1 Henri Fantin-Latour (1836–1904), *Three Peaches on a Plate*, 1868, oil on paper on canvas. Art Reserve / Alamy Stock Photo.

But what made me stand there for some time was not just that it was a realistic depiction of one of my favorite fruits. It was more the feeling that in some sense this painting was teaching me, for the very first time, what makes peaches the way they are, including what makes them look so tasty. Of course, I know what a peach looks like and I can tell when a peach is ripe or not. But it occurred to me that in my past numerous encounters with peaches, I had not been really paying attention to the way a peach appears to me in my own experience.

How many times in our daily lives do we stop and pay attention to the way things appear just in the way they present themselves to us? We often say, "This looks like this and that" or "It appears to me like. . .", but such expressions are followed by, "but in reality, it is such and such." In other words, we use these expressions to refer to the way things appear *in the way they are really not*. We attend to the appearance of things *in this sense* all the time. But how about attending to the way things appear *just in the way they present themselves to us*? Instead of looking at things against our prior knowledge, we refrain from making any judgment and simply let the phenomenon play itself out. How often do we do this?

Not very often. Most of the time, we are involved with our practical engagements, getting things done and satisfying our needs. Whenever I feel like eating a nice juicy fruit, I pick up a ripe peach from the kitchen table, wash it under water and bite into it. Even when I make a judgment, as I sort through the bunch, that the peach is ripe, I'm only attending to how ripe and tasteful it looks and not, for example, to the different variations of color and the textures that are involved in its ripeness.

What was really interesting, as I was standing in front of the painting, was that I felt more present with the peaches than when I am actually holding them in my hands. Usually, when I am just enjoying its taste, I am unaware of what makes the peach look so real and so tasty. I simply take it for granted that they *are* real and tasty. But the painting revealed to me how the various colors, lights, and shadings are all at play in my simple visual perception of a peach. It was an eye-opening experience where I learned that I am normally seeing much less than I think I am. The painting was an invitation to look at the peaches in the way that Latour did—dropping our usual perceptions (which are filtered by our habits and needs) to discover aspects of reality that are otherwise hidden from us. In other words, the painting helped me learn about my habit-bound perceptions and it invited me to play with the appearance of things.[4]

Other forms of art, like music, theater, and literature, can also prompt us to discover more about reality. As you become more and more immersed in these various forms of art, whether as the creator or spectator, there is a sense in which you leave your actual world and are transported to another world. And when you return, so to speak, to your accustomed world, you feel that your actual world has somehow been expanded and your view of things enriched. A great piece of artwork can really change the way you understand reality because great artists know that our usual perceptions are a result of various filters. So even if you're not a great artist yourself, you can benefit from those artists by letting the artworks filter your filters, inviting you to play with your filters, seeing more of reality or seeing reality differently than you usually do. Has any artwork or art experience made you spontaneously fall into the play of the appearance of reality?

Case 4: Playing With Nature

When you look at small children playing outside, spending the whole day building random things out of sticks and stones, it can sometimes make you feel nostalgic for those days when you had a completely different relation to reality. Everything around you was wondrous and nothing was so fixed, not even your identity. There was no single reality, but instead, we would constantly be creating and recreating our realities through pretend play. Now, as grown-ups, we speak as though there is just this one reality where all the "important stuff" happens. Well, here is a case where nature can pull us out of the rigidity of everyday life and bring our natural playfulness back to life.

One day, I was sitting outside with my mentor, Piet Hut, at our usual spot at the Institute for Advanced Study in Princeton where we would have our morning chats. It had been several months since I completed my PhD in Philosophy and I was trying to get a more in-depth understanding of Zen Buddhism, something I had put off during my studies until then. I had started reading Dōgen's works (the Japanese Zen Buddhist priest from the thirteenth century) and Piet and I would chat about Dōgen, Nishida Kitarō (the founder of the Kyoto School), and phenomenology.

Piet saw that I was really struggling with Dōgen. He saw that I was too much in my head. So, he suggested we take a moment to appreciate the presence of appearance, or "APA" as Piet would call it. This was an exercise we often did at the Institute, from my first day there when we took a walk in the woods. After some time, as I let my eyes wander around, letting things present themselves from themselves, something struck me. There, in the middle of the courtyard, I witnessed for the first time, *the dancing leaves*.

My eyes weren't specifically fixed on the tree or on the leaves. But something about the way the leaves were moving demanded my attention. This tree had been there all along and I would go around it every day to get to our place on the other side of the courtyard. I knew it was there. But all this time, I hadn't really cared to look at it. Actually, even if I had, it wouldn't have changed my perception of it in the way that it did then. Normally, I would just look at the tree as a tree, see the leaves moving and maybe say, "Oh, it's quite windy today."

But this time, I wasn't looking at the tree. I was not the subject observing the tree-object. I was also not observing the leaves dancing. The usual subject-object duality that filters all our perceptions was not there. Instead, there were simply "the dancing leaves." I was selflessly present to "the dancing leaves." This is not a metaphor. I don't mean that I saw the leaves moving *as if* they were dancing. I also don't mean that I saw the leaves with dancing legs and arms. I was no longer there as my usual self, but instead I was selflessly present to "the dancing leaves," a phrase that naturally came to me in that very moment.

It was a beautiful moment. So much was happening there. Each leaf was playfully dancing together with the others in perfect coordination, having so much fun. Naturally, I had a smile on my face. My body felt lighter and my mind clearer. And I almost had tears in my eyes. I had been sitting in the same spot almost every day for the last several months. I was seeing the same scene every day. Yet, this was the first time I actually saw the dancing leaves. Why? Why hadn't I noticed this in the past and why did I notice it now?

Unfortunately, many of us are out of touch with nature today. Even when we're surrounded by nature, like in Princeton or in many more places in Japan outside of Tokyo, we're usually so busy and occupied with the things we need to do and get done that nature goes unnoticed. And even when we do have a good relation to it, we usually keep a comfortable distance to it as something that makes us relax, like aroma candles or a nice massage. Even then, they are things for us to use. But in that moment when I saw the dancing leaves, this accustomed relation dissipated. Instead, there were simply the dancing leaves. The dancing leaves were not there to serve my needs. A much more fundamental relation between nature and us human beings revealed itself. I felt connected, that I was part of the vast play of nature. Even after some time had passed, I was still sitting there with a sense of wonder and awe. And I realized that, as small children, we used to be able to play with nature like this all the time. But as we became adults and learned how serious and important human life is, we forgot our essential connection to nature. We forgot how to play with nature.

Fortunately, nature is still around us. You don't need to try to become a child again to get back in touch with your playfulness. And not only is this unnecessary, but it is also undesirable. Trying to revert back to being children would only amount to becoming childish, irresponsible adults. What we need to do instead is to tap into that basic connection that is already there by tuning into the way nature plays. You'll then eventually forget that you're at the center of reality and naturally recover your playfulness that allows you to be in harmony with nature. This requires much practice and discipline, something that in itself requires a kind of maturity, and the result would be a higher sense of playing with nature that is very much responsible to both ourselves and to nature. But a good place to start is to recall some examples from your own experience where you spontaneously fell into the play of nature like I did. What was your experience like?

Discussion Questions

- What are some examples of the "culturally colored glasses" that you might have? Can you suspend them to some extent, temporarily?
- Can you recall instances from your own experience where the discussion was not playing itself out? This is usually accompanied by a sense that the discussion did not go so well. What do you think kept it from playing itself out?

- Different forms of art can make us aware of our various filters and habits. When this happens, it is often accompanied by a sense of surprise and perhaps even a shock. What are some of the filters that are brought to light after listening to a wonderful piece of music? How about after reading your favorite literature? And after attending an enthralling performance at a theater?
- To be responsible here means that one is responsive to nature by playing with nature. How does this sense of responsibility compare to our usual sense of responsibility that we associate with accountability, duty, and blame? Where does the sense of this latter kind of responsibility emanate from?

3

Openness, Playfulness, and Freedom

In this chapter, we will go through some ideas of philosophers and thinkers that have contributed significantly to the development of the idea of the epoché that I am presenting in this book. By giving you a picture of who and what is behind the idea, my hope is for you to get a better understanding of my version of the epoché as a way to play with reality. Having this background understanding will help you with the exercises in the following chapter, as this present chapter provides the theoretical basis for the kind of exploration we will be doing in Chapter 4. But if you prefer to go straight into the exercises, you can skip this chapter. That is also okay. I would only advise that you come back to this chapter afterwards to help you see some of the nuances that the exercises help bring about.

The obvious place to start is Edmund Husserl (1859–1938), the father of phenomenology. As I briefly mentioned in Chapter 1, the original source of the idea of the epoché you find in this book is Husserl's "phenomenological epoché." We'll see in detail below but the most important point that is common to both Husserl's original version and my version of the epoché is the idea that the epoché is essentially a method of cultivating an *openness* towards phenomena, namely the appearance of things just in the way they present themselves to us. But as I also mentioned before, my version of the epoché does not coincide with Husserl's original version. While taking over important aspects of it, I have essentially given it a more practical spin by presenting it as a useful tool not just for phenomenologists but for anyone who is willing to make use of it in their everyday life.

What you will discover in this chapter is that such an interpretation of the epoché did not come out of nowhere but in fact finds ground in other neighboring sources to Husserl's phenomenology. One such source is the hermeneutic phenomenology of Hans-Georg Gadamer (1900–2002) and Paul Ricoeur (1913–2005). This may be somewhat surprising for some people since neither of them were really interested in Husserl's notion of the phenomenological epoché (nor in working out a specific method for phenomenology). However, as we will see, their practical conceptions of phenomenology are much more in line with my own understanding of it and their emphasis on the idea of play in human understanding is especially

Figure 2 Portrait of Edmund Husserl (1859–1938). Mondadori Publishers, Public domain, via Wikimedia Commons.

insightful. While neither Gadamer nor Ricoeur claimed to be providing a new interpretation of the phenomenological epoché, it is interesting to see how far we could explore the idea of playing with reality if we bring together their notion of *playfulness* with the kind of openness that we cultivate through the phenomenological epoché.

Another source I draw from is the philosophy of the modern Japanese philosopher and father of the Kyoto School tradition, Nishida Kitarō (西田幾多郎 1870–1945). This may come as more of a surprise since neither Nishida scholars nor phenomenologists consider Nishida to be a phenomenologist. In fact, Nishida himself was rather critical of Husserl's whole phenomenological program. But this is not because he disagreed with Husserl's interest in all that purely presents itself in our experience. He shared this basic focus with Husserl. Nishida's main insight was to radicalize the idea of phenomena from Husserl's idea of the appearance of something to someone, to the presentation of reality beyond the subject-object duality. As a matter of fact, as we will see below, Nishida's search for a reality beyond the subject-object duality is traditional in Japanese thought. We find similar lines of thinking (or *non*-thinking) in the haiku poet Matsuo Bashō. Both of them talk about dropping the standpoint that assumes the subject-object duality and tuning into the natural unfolding of non-dual reality. This gives rise to a kind of *freedom* that allows us to enjoy the play of reality while avoiding identifying with any of the roles that are being played. Even though Nishida did not show any particular interest in the phenomenological epoché, if we understand Nishida to be inviting us to do a radical epoché by bracketing the subject-object duality that is ingrained in our ways of understanding reality, we can see this as an invitation to explore a whole new dimension of openness and playfulness that is coupled with a new level of freedom.

Husserl: Openness to Phenomena

Edmund Husserl's philosophical project was to clarify the essential structures of our experience. He did this not by appealing to logical arguments or by introducing some theory of the mind. Rather, the general principle, which he called the "principle of all principles," was to appeal to what is directly given to us in our experience just as it presents itself to us, nothing more and nothing less.[1] But this is easier said than done. First of all, usually when we are involved in our practical lives, we are more focused on the various objects and people we deal with and less attentive to our own experiences of them. Therefore we say, "He's very old-fashioned," attributing old-fashionedness to the person as if it's an objective trait without reflecting on the process in which we made this judgment based on how the person originally presented himself to us in our experience. Second, as soon as we ask ourselves how things present themselves to us, we start appealing to various psychological theories and new findings in neuroscience that explain how the mind and the brain functions. And as soon as we do that, we leave the domain of what is directly given to us in our experience.

In order to secure the field of "phenomena," namely the appearance of things just in the way they present themselves to us, Husserl introduced a method that allowed him to distance from various theories that attempt to explain how we experience the world. This was called the "phenomenological epoché." It is the method of suspending judgment on the basic belief which all theories of the mind assume, namely the belief in the existence of the world and the objects in it. In doing so, we do not doubt their existence. We also neither affirm nor deny. As Husserl would say, we "bracket" or "put out of play" the belief in the existence of objects and the world.[2]

Once we have suspended judgment regarding the existence of objects and the world, we can re-engage with them in a new light. Husserl called this re-engagement the "phenomenological reduction." "Reduction" here doesn't mean "diminish in size," but it means that it is a kind of "leading back" (from the Latin, *re-* "back" and *ducere* "lead") to the phenomena. Importantly, we don't get rid of objects and the world in the process of the reduction since we don't negate their existence but only suspend judgment regarding the status of their existence. So, it is not that phenomenology somehow deals only with our mental experience, leaving the external world out of the picture (a common misunderstanding of phenomenology). Phenomenology is not psychology per se (though it could be a method for psychology as we find in phenomenological psychology). Rather, phenomenology is a study of objects and the world, just not in the straightforward manner that assumes their existence. Since phenomenology takes the extra step of suspending judgment regarding their existence, it is a study of objects and the world *insofar as they present themselves in our experience.*

As a method of bracketing the perennial metaphysical question regarding the existence of the world, you may think that the epoché is concerned with a highly philosophical problem (in the sense of being very abstract and far-removed from everyday practical concerns). Yet we must not forget that for Husserl the epoché was a method of going back to the phenomena themselves, as his slogan for phenomenology, "Back to the things themselves!", asserts. Husserl's primary interest was not in bracketing the metaphysical question of whether or not the world really exists. Rather, it was in the phenomenologically reduced (in the above sense) realm, namely all that directly presents itself to us in our experience. His interest was therefore much more concrete. The epoché was simply a method that would allow access to this direct experience.

The phenomenological re-engagement with this direct experience broadens the scope of what we can see and understand. One may think the opposite because it makes us take up a specific perspective, namely the phenomenological, on the field of phenomena that has been isolated through the epoché and reduction. But the phenomenological epoché and reduction are reflective methods that essentially let us see more. In this respect, they are quite similar to the way we come to see more through art, as in my example of Latour's peaches from the last chapter. Both the phenomenological and the aesthetic attitudes are ways of discovering those aspects of reality that are usually covered up by our practical concerns. Their means of expressing the discovered reality differ and so do their aims, but both the phenomenologist and the artist know that we are usually seeing much less than what reality actually has to offer.

The phenomenological epoché and reduction can open us up to engage with the world in a way that is free from the basic assumption that colors most of our engagements. This is the assumption that the external world is out there, existing apart from us. This assumption seduces us with the usual baggage which our sense of "existing" usually carries, namely "existing as such and such" or "existing in the way we know of." In this way, we are always smuggling in many of our hidden beliefs under the cover of our understanding of "existing." When we set aside this powerful filter, to which we are usually not aware that it is a filter, we can begin to play with the phenomena. We can begin to let the phenomena show themselves from themselves.

Through this phenomenological perspective, we can study the different ways things can appear to us in our experience. We can see how imagining a face differs from having a perception of a face in front of you. For example, while the imagined face disappears if I stop imagining it, the perceived face will remain regardless of my perceiving it. As we go through this kind of process, we can begin to extract the invariant patterns, or what Husserl called the "essences," of our various experiences. Essences are the structures of a phenomenon without which it would not be that phenomenon. They are not mysterious things that are hidden somewhere behind our experiences. Rather, they can be directly apprehended by us in our experiences. One of the essences of imagination, and not of perception, may be that the imagining consciousness "produces and conserves the object as imaged" as Jean-Paul Sartre maintained.[3] In this way the image is dependent on the imagining consciousness. But in order for us to really call this an essence, we would have to go through a whole range of imaginary experiences and check the results with other phenomenologists. Phenomenology is therefore thoroughly empirical and scientific in the sense that it relies on the method of reproducibility of experiments by peer phenomenologists.

As we go deeper into the phenomenological analysis of our relation to the world, we begin to realize something remarkable about our experience. Namely, we realize that the world would not be what it is without our experience or consciousness. Consciousness gives the world meaning. We are not Gods that create the world. But we do create and cognize the meanings of the world, without which the world would simply not be what it is. This may be surprising since we like to think that the world is what it is regardless of our existence. But even the objective facts about the world that sciences reveal have their objective meaning only because consciousness is there to disclose them. In this way, Husserl discovered the sense-giving consciousness or subjectivity (he called this "transcendental subjectivity") at the base of our relation to the world.

Husserl's discovery of transcendental subjectivity has some things in common with Descartes' discovery of the "cogito" or the thinking subject. While Descartes' methodological doubt is not the same as Husserl's method of bracketing, both methods were employed towards the aim of discovering the foundation upon which our knowledge and experience of the world would be based. But the main difference between Descartes and Husserl is that the former sought the cogito as the first principle upon which everything else could be based, while for Husserl consciousness was no absolute foundation where all philosophical inquiry could come to an end (even though he would sometimes refer to the meaning-bestowing consciousness as "absolute"). For Husserl, phenomenology is an open-ended endeavor that seeks to ground our relation to the world in the essential structures of our experience. It is open-ended because such an endeavor requires us to constantly check with our experience and with each other whether we have got the phenomena right. The phenomenological standpoint is therefore essentially driven by the motive to understand phenomena for their own sake. It demands an openness towards phenomena.

But although the phenomenological perspective is an open perspective, it is a rather specific and narrow one. The phenomenological perspective is not only about openness towards phenomena, but it is equally about finding the invariant patterns of our experience (this is called the "eidetic reduction"). And for Husserl, this was all for the purpose of establishing phenomenology as the foundational science of all sciences. Therefore, when the phenomenological epoché is presented as part of such a specific program, the potential scope of the epoché is inevitably narrowed down. It becomes less of a practical tool for everyone's daily use and more of a technical tool for specialists only.

Of course, putting it this way is somewhat odd since it was never Husserl's intention to narrow down the scope of the epoché. The epoché in its original form was introduced as a specific tool for phenomenologists. My point is that this was somewhat unfortunate, for the original form was unnecessarily limited to the phenomenological program that Husserl envisioned. We can broaden its sense by taking it out of the specific context in which it originally developed and putting it instead in a different, more practical context. Importantly, I do not believe this is an arbitrary move. The essence of the phenomenological epoché is not something that should be of interest to phenomenologists only. We can all benefit from opening up to the way things present themselves just as they appear to us. By adopting such a perspective, we can learn how limiting our usual ways of seeing are and begin to see more than before. For phenomenologists, this is the first step to further inquire into the "essences" of our experience. For the rest of us, who are not phenomenologists, this can be the first step towards playing with reality.

Gadamer and Ricoeur: Understanding is Playing

While Husserl's primary interest in phenomenology was for the purpose of fulfilling his ideal of philosophy as a rigorous and foundational science, his hermeneutic followers had a rather different approach to phenomenology. For Hans-Georg Gadamer and Paul Ricoeur, who developed what they call "hermeneutic phenomenology" (which was a direction of phenomenology Martin Heidegger opened up), phenomenology was primarily a way of interpreting and understanding the historical meanings that are present in cultural media, both linguistic (like written texts) and non-linguistic (like art). And since interpretation and understanding are not only concerns for the sciences but important for human experience in general, the main interest of hermeneutic phenomenology was less specific and much more practice-oriented than Husserl's scientific vision of phenomenology.

Gadamer was specifically interested in articulating the conditions of our understanding. What makes understanding possible? For Gadamer,

Figure 3 Portrait of Hans-Georg Gadamer (1900–2002). dpa picture alliance / Alamy Stock Photo.

understanding occurs in our engagements with the unfamiliar, whether it is in reading texts, encountering other traditions, or engaging in a dialogue with others. Sticking with the last case, the general aim of a dialogue is to reach a common or better understanding of a subject matter. But this would not be achieved if the interlocutors are not willing to hear something other than what they already know. In other words, for a dialogue to be possible, you must be willing to listen and to learn something new from the other. You must engage in the dialogue with an openness towards the other.

But this kind of engagement requires that you are also willing to change your views if the dialogue presents a better understanding of the subject matter. You must then take a distance from your prejudices (in the sense of pre-judgments or, as Gadamer defines it, "a judgment that is rendered before all the elements that determine a situation have been finally examined"[4]) by letting the dialogue guide you rather than the other way around. Of course, in a sense the interlocutors do guide the dialogue by bringing in their perspectives. But neither of them should have control over the dialogue. As soon as you try to control the dialogue, you are no longer genuinely listening to the other or are exposing your prejudices. Only when you let the dialogue guide you and listen to what the other has to say will you become aware of your prejudices as prejudices. And if they turn out to be inadequate, for the dialogue to be fruitful, you must be willing to let go of them or adjust them and re-engage with the dialogue from a new perspective. In this way, the understanding involved in a dialogue involves a back-and-forth movement between distancing from your own prejudices and re-engaging from the new perspective.[5]

Gadamer has called this movement of the understanding, the "play" of understanding.[6] When one engages in understanding, whether it is in understanding a text or another person, one is playing. This doesn't mean that understanding is not a serious matter. When you play a game, you would be a spoilsport if you don't take it seriously. You must submit to the rules of the game and hand yourself over to the world of the game. Therefore, when we seriously play, we are actually suspending judgment on our commitment to our "real," practical worlds and letting a different world come into play. Likewise, when we engage in understanding, we must bracket our commitments to our own standpoints and immerse ourselves in the play of understanding. As a player of understanding, you cannot control its rules and course of direction. As Gadamer would say, when you play you are being played by the game.[7]

Ricoeur takes Gadamer's analysis of play as a guide to understanding how distancing and re-engaging take place in reading or writing a work of fiction or poetry.[8] According to Ricoeur, understanding the meaning of a

Figure 4 Portrait of Paul Ricoeur (1913–2005). Sueddeutsche Zeitung Photo / Alamy Stock Photo.

text cannot be accomplished by imposing one's own understanding onto the text. In the context of reading, he calls this the "narcissism of the reader" where one finds only oneself in the text.[9] Instead, one must expose oneself and let the text speak for itself. And as it speaks to you, you can then begin to find your own understanding of it. This process of understanding, which is a kind of play, is even more radical in the case of reading fiction and poetry.

When we read a novel, Ricoeur tells us that we must distance ourselves from the meaning horizons of our everyday lives in order to engage with the imaginary world of the text. And as we get immersed in the imaginary world, we start acquiring a new meaning horizon that has opened up in and through the text. Ricoeur has called this process "distanciation" and "appropriation" respectively. Distanciation is the bracketing of our everyday worlds and appropriation is to make one's own what was initially an alien world.[10]

An important part of this interplay is that we also let go of our usual self and acquire a renewed self. Therefore, as a reader of fiction, one becomes a playful figure that puts on identities like we normally do with clothes. As we leave our actual world, we take off our worn-out clothes and put on new ones we receive from the imaginary world. In this way, engaging with fiction involves playing with our self-understandings, which is very much a part of how we understand reality.

In the last chapter, I mentioned the story of how my upbringing has allowed me to create a distance from the two cultures I was brought up in. Back when I was growing-up, I wasn't always happy living in between the two cultures. I didn't feel at home in either of them, and I didn't know where I belonged. This was a very serious and existential problem I had for a very long time. But thanks to the experience, I now have a very different way of looking at it. I still don't know who I really am, and I never know how to answer to a typical question I often get asked, "Do you feel more Japanese or American?" But the difference is that I don't feel anxious about not knowing what culture I belong to. On the contrary, I enjoy playing different roles! I no longer feel the need to identify myself as either American or Japanese, or even as a Japanese-American or an American-Japanese. Instead, I take these cultural identities as something I can play with (and not something I *am*). Of course, our cultures are not fictional. They are what actually characterize human beings as human beings. Nonetheless, just as we need to let go of our actual world in order to dwell in a fictional world, so we need to let go of our own cultural standpoints in order to have a living understanding of another culture. It is interesting that the latter is usually much more difficult to do in practice than the former. We are somehow more willing to give up our actual world to dwell in an imaginary world than to dwell in a different living culture. How odd is that! But perhaps the key is to try engaging in another culture in the way we do with fiction: forget who we are and to completely immerse ourselves in the other world.

It is interesting that Ricoeur explicitly makes a connection between the Husserlian idea of the epoché and his idea of distanciation.[11] This is interesting because it suggests that Ricoeur was also supportive of the idea of broadening the scope of the Husserlian epoché. But what is even more interesting is his understanding of appropriation. For Ricoeur, appropriation does not consist in the subject projecting meaning onto the text from his or her own prior understanding. It is also not about trying to recover and identify with the understanding of the original audience of the text. On the contrary, there is what he calls a "letting-go" or "relinquishment of the subject" in appropriation.[12] The subject, namely the reader, must let go of the ego's grasping of meaning and instead, let the meaning of the text reveal itself from itself. Only then is appropriation accomplished in a genuine sense. Appropriation therefore implies a "dispossession of the narcissistic *ego*."[13]

An important point that both Gadamer and Ricoeur underline is how understanding involves letting go of control and becoming playful in turn. This means that if we want to seriously understand another text, tradition, or a person for its own sake, then we must loosen our grip on our commitments to our views and positions and begin playing with understanding. And most importantly, if we are to seriously play, then we must realize that as players of understanding, we are not in charge of the game. As Gadamer would say, the subject of play is not the players but the play itself.[14] So to play with understanding is to let the understanding play itself out.

If we recall the case of how I lost myself in the topic of discussion, as we saw in Chapter 2, the above discussion suggests that this was a case where genuine understanding was happening. The more I became immersed in the topic, the more I became less self-absorbed and more playful. There was a letting go of the anxious ego as I became more and more engaged in the discussion. And as the group dynamics got better, there was a sense that the discussion had a life of its own, playing itself out. No one was trying to control the course of the discussion, but instead, everyone had left their little egos and was letting the topic guide them. We were all playing with understanding in the sense that there was the presence of the play of understanding.

Nishida: Letting Go of Thinking

In their emphasis on the notion of play, Gadamer and Ricoeur went a long way towards removing the subjectivistic tendencies of Husserlian phenomenology. In the context of the epoché, Gadamer and Ricoeur provide us with some hints to explore how playfulness comes to feature as we bracket our strong belief in the subject reigning over reality. In this last section, the Japanese philosopher Nishida Kitarō will help us take further steps in this direction. We will see how Nishida's invitation to do a radical epoché will open us up to a whole new dimension of openness and playfulness as well as a new level of freedom.

As I mentioned earlier, Nishida's relation to phenomenology was almost exclusively polemical. This is somewhat surprising considering the fact that Nishida shared the phenomenological interest in all that directly presents itself in our experience. And like Husserl, Nishida too believed that we need to take some extra steps to secure this field of phenomena. But what was truly radical about Nishida's move is that instead of suspending judgment, he suspended *reflection*.[15] However radical Husserl's suspension of judgment was, it didn't bracket the very means of doing philosophy. Nishida went so far as to suspend the very method of philosophy. His method was: *stop reflecting and let things unfold on their own*.

But again, this is easier said than done.[16] Just as we have a natural tendency to assume that the world is out there, reflecting on our experience is also part

Figure 5 Portrait of Nishida Kitarō (1870–1945). The Asahi Shimbun Company / amanaimages.

of our nature. When I reflect on my experience, say, of seeing a flower, I set up a divide between the subject and the object. I become aware of myself, the subject, who is looking at the flower, the object. Once this subject is established, it wants to think that it was always there even prior to reflection. That is the power of reflection! It interprets the original experience as already divided into the subject-object duality.

When we suspend reflection and try to let things unfold on their own, unless we are very careful and attentive, we are always sneaking in this subject-object framework. We say, prior to reflection, there is just *the appearance of the flower.* But in putting it this way, we are already assuming that the flower, the object, is appearing to you, the subject. From Nishida's standpoint, Husserl was still assuming this point even when he bracketed the existence of objects and the world. For Husserl, phenomena were always an experience *of* something *for* someone (Husserl called this "intentionality"). When Nishida suspends reflection, he is suggesting that we suspend intentionality. In doing so, not only is he taking a distance to our activity of reflection, but he is also distancing from this subject-object duality that pervades much of our way of understanding experience.

Any kind of linguistic articulation has its limits when it comes to expressing this "pure experience," as Nishida called it, that breaks the subject-object duality.[17] But Nishida puts it quite aptly when he says that in the very moment of seeing a flower, "I am the flower, the flower is me."[18] We would be missing the point if we take this as a metaphorical use of language. If it was metaphorical, we would be assuming that I am *not* the flower, and the flower is *not* me; we are separate entities. Rather, as an expression of pure experience, this phrase should be taken seriously. In that very experience, when a small flower grasped his whole being, his usual sense that I am looking at the flower dropped. Instead, the flower was simply doing its own thing, blooming away and waiting for another breeze. Nishida was not there anymore, at least not as the subject of the experience. Yet "he" was fully present and tuned in to the natural unfolding of the flower. In that sense he was the flower, and the flower was him.

Nishida's understanding of "true reality" as the experience of reality beyond the subject-object duality is actually native to traditional Japanese thought. There is a famous line from Matsuo Bashō, a haiku poet from the seventeenth century, that reads: "From the pine tree learn of the pine tree, and from the bamboo of the bamboo."[19] What is expressed here is essentially what Nishida is trying to get at with his idea of pure experience. When we try to understand what a pine tree is, we usually examine its properties, how it relates to its environment, etc. In short, we examine it as an object. But Bashō suggests that we should abandon such a standpoint if we want to really know what a pine tree is. The subject-object duality must be dropped.

What we should do instead is to take up the standpoint of the pine tree. But not as an object, as that would again assume the subject-object duality. As Nishida would say, we "become the thing" (*mono to naru* 物となる).[20] Nishitani Keiji, one of Nishida's disciples, called this the "standpoint of *śūnyata* (or emptiness)."[21] It is the standpoint where the subject has given away its central position as the knower to the thing itself. When we are selflessly open to the pine tree, the pine tree shows its way of being settled in its own position, naturally unfolding according to its own way of being. Instead of trying to grasp it as an object, we let go of this grasp, and simply let the thing appear from within itself. Therefore, taking up the standpoint of the pine tree (or the standpoint of emptiness) means that we become attuned to the voice of the thing and speak from its standpoint. The nature of the pine tree is revealed to us from this standpoint.

In the same spirit, Bashō also made a distinction between two kinds of haiku, "*suru-ku*" (する句) and "*naru-ku*" (なる句).[22] "*Suru-ku*," which literally means doing-poem, is the kind of haiku that is created through one's conscious efforts after days of thinking, writing, and rewriting. For Bashō, such haiku in fact does not amount to good haiku. Rather, good haiku arises from the elimination of one's will and one's subjective coloring of the experience. He calls such haiku "*naru-ku*," literally meaning becoming-poem. Such poetry is created when one forgets that one is trying to create a haiku and the poem spontaneously develops on its own, so to speak. A similar kind of thing can happen in writing an essay or thinking about some urgent problem. Sometimes when a new idea comes out, we are led to say, "the idea just came to me" and we are often surprised by the new idea. There is a sense that it came from somewhere other than you, that you were not really the creator of the idea. These occasions often occur after spending days of hard work and effort. After being frustrated with yourself for the inability to produce anything new, you let go of all that tension built around your will to create. Then, as if it was just waiting for the right timing to come out, the idea

Figure 6 Calligraphy of "*mu*" (無, nothingness) by Nishida (year unknown). On the left is written Nishida's *kojigō* (居士号, a name given to a Buddhist layman), "*sunshin*" (寸心). Nishida wrote several different versions of "*mu*" (無), but this one stands out in its resemblance to a person in *zazen*. You can get a sense that this work was created in a spontaneous way similar to what Bashō calls "*naru-ku*" in poetry. *Nishida Kitarō Ibokushū*, Tōeisha, No. 87. Public Domain.

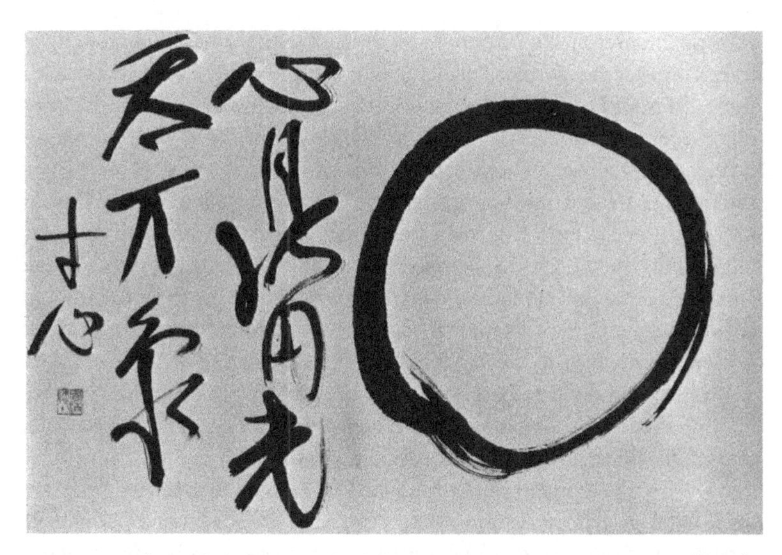

Figure 7 Calligraphy of the words of the Zen Master Banzan Hōshaku (盤山宝積) by Nishida from 1935. It reads: "*Shingetsukoen hikari banzo o nomu*" (心月孤円光呑万象) meaning, "The perfect circle of the mind-moon is alone. Its light swallows myriad phenomena." *Nishida Kitarō Ibokushū*, Tōeisha. Public Domain.

is born. "*Naru-ku*," or the kind of poem that spontaneously comes to be, without our doing, can then be said to be expressive of what Nishida calls "pure experience" or what Nishitani calls the "standpoint of emptiness."

An important point is that for these Japanese thinkers, tuning in to the voice of the things is not just a matter of knowing the nature of the things, but it is also about knowing our own nature as human beings. The two points go together. In Japanese, the word for "according to our own will" (*mizukara*, 自ら) and "according to its own way of being" (*onozukara*, 自ずから) employ the same Chinese character, "自" (*ji*). In English, we use the word "will" or "freewill" to refer to the former and clearly distinguish this from how things "naturally" occur. Since the Japanese saw an inherent connection between the two, it was only natural for them to use a single character and separate the meanings according to the way it was read. Of course, the Japanese knew that the two senses can come apart and that most of the time, the way we act according to our own will is not in accordance with the natural unfolding of things. But for the ancient Japanese, we are also usually not really free. For them, the most fundamental sense of freedom is realized when our will drops off and we are attuned to the reality which is beyond the subject-object duality. The nature of both things and ourselves is revealed in such a standpoint. We are most free when we are playing with reality. Or put differently, we are most free when we let reality play itself out.[23]

A similar tendency can be observed in how the Japanese today speak about important events in life. When one wants to notify their friends and co-workers about their recent marriage, one would formally say, "*konotabiwa kekkon suru hakobi to narimashita*" (この度は結婚する運びとなりました), which literally translates to, "things have developed such that we have become married." You may say: "What a passive way of speaking about such important events in life!" Indeed, even when the marriage was something that was decided upon by the two people, it is common to speak of important life events in general as something that has happened out of a natural movement of events, rather than something that was actively brought about by us. Whether or not people today still have an actual living sense of this is another question (and I think a serious one we should be addressing), but the language suggests a deep sense of unity between the way we make important life decisions and the way things naturally come to be. When people speak in this manner with some degree of awareness of the language, it is often accompanied by an appreciation for the natural unfolding of events. The couple may not have gotten married without the will of the two, but if they hadn't met to begin with or if the timing wasn't quite right, both of which are beyond our control, the possibility of marriage would have not been in their hands to begin with. There is a sense that we are at the mercy of a greater force called "nature" and to be free is to not be free from it but to actively take part in it.

Looking back at the case of the dancing leaves from the last chapter, we can say that this was certainly an instance of pure experience. When the dancing leaves revealed themselves, the usual subject-object duality dropped off. I was no longer there looking at the leaves. There were simply the dancing leaves. I was not looking at the dancing leaves, but instead, "I" was selflessly open to the play of nature. I was freed from the self-enclosed ego that was confused and concerned about understanding the words of the great Zen Buddhist priest. There was so much happening in front of my eyes, and I felt part of this play. It was a truly liberating moment.

This kind of experience is not very common in our everyday life since in the process of growing-up, it has become the default position to see reality through the subject-object duality. This is probably one of our most closely worn colored glasses. Nishida's philosophy was about clarifying how, despite our natural tendency to stay within the subject-object framework, pure experience is the "true reality" that lies at the ground of our relation to the world. And since this true reality is neither subject nor object, this ground is not an absolute foundation, and it cannot be called subjectivity. Instead, it is the pure openness of the groundless ground.

At the core of Nishida's thinking lies the Zen Buddhist-inspired idea that non-thinking is the key to understanding reality. Yet as a philosopher, he was not content to simply accept that. Instead, he sought to articulate this basic insight through reflection and thinking. This is how we get the paradoxical invitation from a philosopher to suspend reflection. This is indeed quite a challenging invitation. Suspending judgment about the existence of the world was already an unnatural move that requires discipline and persistence. Suspending reflection and letting reality play itself out is even more demanding since most of the time we don't even realize that we are seeing reality through the lens of the subject-object duality. It is especially challenging for academic philosophers for whom taking a distance from reflection and conceptual articulation would even be considered as a threat to their discipline. In truth it is both difficult and quite simple. How difficult is it to drop our commitment to our standpoints and play with understanding as Gadamer and Ricoeur suggested? It might seem difficult when we think about it and try to intellectually understand what this really means. But when we let understanding play itself out, like we do when we genuinely engage in a dialogue, we naturally become open and playful. What Nishida is suggesting is not so dissimilar. If we just let ourselves tune in to the natural rhythm of things, whether it is the pine tree or our interpersonal relationships, and stop trying to make it into something it is not or control its course of development, then the play of reality will reveal itself quite naturally. And we'll happily find ourselves to be more open, playful, and freer than before.

Discussion Questions

- Compare Husserl's phenomenological epoché with Descartes' methodological doubt. Both methods involve changing the way we relate to our commonly held belief in the external world. Can you find some similarities and differences in the way they do this?
- Ricoeur talked about "distancing" or bracketing our everyday world in order to dwell in the fictional world. We do something similar when we bracket our cultural beliefs and perspectives in order to understand another culture for its own sake. But it is often easier to set aside our

everyday world to live in the fictional world than to bracket our cultural beliefs to see the world from another cultural standpoint. Do you agree? If yes, why do you think this is the case? If not, what is your experience of the two cases?

- We saw how Nishida not only applied the epoché to our judgments and beliefs, but also to the activity of philosophical reflection itself (where such reflection is central to doing philosophy). He also says reflection still assumes a "subject-object" duality. Can you see how this is true, at least in theory? Can you also see examples of it in your own ways of experiencing life?

4

Practicing Playing

In Chapter 2, we looked at a few cases where I spontaneously fell into the play of reality to help you find your own examples of where you fell into the play. Then in Chapter 3, we covered the philosophical background to the specific idea of the epoché I am presenting in this book. In this chapter, we will finally practice playing with reality. You will find three main exercises that are designed to target specific aspects of the epoché to help us play with reality in different ways. Each exercise is followed by some observations that bring up various points that you may notice during the exercises. It is recommended that you only read over the observation after you have done the exercise and made some observations yourself. So, pick up a pen and notebook and let's get started!

Exercise 1: Playing with Imagination

In this exercise, which is a series of small exercises, we will play with our imagination. No need to take it too seriously, just try to enjoy yourself while you're at it. The most important thing is to have fun.

First, take a moment to look around your surroundings. Then bring your attention back to yourself and where you are right now, whether you are sitting, standing up, or lying down. Perhaps your mind has already started imagining things as soon as you saw the word "imagination." Or perhaps your mind is wandering somewhere else like on that chocolate ice cream waiting impatiently for you in the freezer. Whatever your mind is doing, try to bring it back to this moment. Try to focus on what is purely given to you in your perceptual experience right now. What do you see? Do you hear anything? And how do you feel? Once you feel that your sense of presence has strengthened—in the sense that you're not somewhere else but right here—you are ready to do the first exercise.

1.1

Imagine that suddenly, out of nowhere, a unicorn appears right in front of you. Try to imagine this unicorn as vividly as possible. How big is it? Is it colorful? What kind of texture does its surface have? Is it moving around or standing still? Sit back or lay back, relax and set your imagination free. Close your eyes if it's easier for you to imagine that way. Take a minute or two to imagine this unicorn in minute detail. Let it really present itself to you. And feel its presence in your imagination.

As you imagine this, also note what has changed in your experience. How has your experience of the world changed once this imaginary unicorn appeared in your experience? And do you feel any different after bringing in this imaginary creature into being?

1.2

Now, imagine that you are riding on the unicorn's back and flying with it (yes, it's a flying unicorn!). If you are sitting inside, let it take you through the walls and over the houses and buildings. If you are outside, jump on its back and see where it takes you. What can you see from there? How does it feel? Will you go higher up in the sky, or will you have a nice ride through the woods? Perhaps you can even communicate with your unicorn. What will you ask the unicorn to do? Play with this imagination for at least three minutes.

As you play with this, bring up the same questions again: What has changed in your experience? How has your experience of the world changed now that you are flying on the back of the unicorn? Do you feel any different from the way you felt before doing this imaginary exercise? And what about compared to when you were just imagining a unicorn in front of you? In what way do you feel different?

1.3

Finally, imagine that you *are* the unicorn. You are no longer whoever you were before, but you have taken up the identity of a unicorn. You can freely fly and go wherever you want in whatever way you want. Explore your new identity. What does it feel like to be a unicorn? Can people see you or are you invisible? How do you interact with your peer unicorns? Play with this imagination for a few more minutes.

As you imagine yourself being a unicorn, ask yourself once again: "What has changed in my experience?" "Now that I am a unicorn, how is my world different from the pre-imaginary world and the two other imaginary worlds of 1.1 and 1.2? How do I feel having taken up a completely new identity of a totally different sort of being from my actual self?"

1.4

Now, stop imagining and come back to where you were before. Put an end to this fun play of your imagination and bring your attention back to what is actually present in your experience. Your imaginary world will probably keep coming back, but try to just stay with your perceptual experience. Do this for half a minute and ask yourself: What has happened in my experience? What feels "more real," my imaginary world or the actual world?

Observations

The main purpose of this series of small exercises was for you to gain a sense of freedom from the ties to the actual world (i.e., the world of our practical lives) as well as to your actual self (the self that gets involved with our practical lives). Playing with your imagination was a way to help you get a sense of this freedom.

In 1.1, as you imagined a unicorn suddenly appear in front of you, an opening was created in your actual world. The more you were present in your perceptual experience before doing the exercise, the more you would have felt the contrast before and after the unicorn appeared. The actual world was no longer your only world. Now you had an imaginary world within the actual world. At this point, you were already a bit freer from your ties to the actual world. But perhaps you didn't feel this so much yet.

When we moved to 1.2 and you started flying on the unicorn's back, a further change occurred. Now, the imaginary world had become part of your world. As you were flying with the unicorn, you began participating in that opening that was created in your actual world. You gained new possibilities that were before mere possibilities of your imaginary being. Those possibilities became part of your own possibilities. But perhaps some of those possibilities were constrained by the possibilities of your actual self. You were participating in the imaginary world, but you hadn't wholly given up your actual world. You were probably the same actual self as before—same name, personal history, job, worries, and so on. The boundary between the imaginary and the actual world was getting a bit blurry but it was still there. But compared to before, you probably felt much more freedom, having gained the ability to fly!

Then at 1.3, you finally *became* the unicorn. You took up a whole new identity. And in doing so, you were also moving into a whole new world. Everything around you was new to you because you took on a new identity with a completely new way of being. The way you perceive and move around the world, interact with others, and even the way you understand yourself were all new. These new possibilities were completely imaginary, based on your own imagination. Not only did you loosen up ties to the actual world, but you also loosened up ties to your concrete, actual self. You were effectively living in a world of pure possibilities. How much freer were you compared to the kind of freedom you have when you identify yourself as "this human being" with "such and such name" having "this or that job"? How far could you get lost in your imagination? Was there a part of you that kept reminding you that this is just your imagination?

This series of exercises is similar to stretching. Just as stretching your body can make you physically flexible over time, playing with our imagination can make us more mentally flexible. As children we were much more flexible, both physically and mentally, and stretching and imagination can help us regain that freedom of the body and the mind respectively. But when you stopped imagining in 1.4, you most likely came back to reality. This sense of "coming back to reality" is the sense that our actual self and the world are what is "real." The actual world is that world in which we do stuff that is important to us. It's the world that matters to us. The actual self is that self we identify with our name and to which we put a lot of effort in giving attention and taking care of. The imaginary world is fun, and it can be very real while we're in it, but once we get out of it, we come back to the actual world, which is "our reality." In this sense, this series of exercises helps you get a bit flexible but not enough to change your mind about what counts as "real." But it's still a good stretching exercise to prepare us for something a bit more challenging.

Exercise 2: Playing with Perception

In this series of exercises, we'll take a step further and see if we can further open ourselves up and become even freer than what imagination alone could allow. We'll see if we can change our sense of the "real" by playing with our perception.

2.1

First, observe what is around you. If it is a place you are familiar with, remind yourself what is around you with all the objects and the meanings they have for you. If it is a new place, let yourself become acquainted with the surroundings. Once you've done that, imagine that everything around you is a very realistic painting of those things. Imagine that you have somehow stepped into a room where all the walls have been painted with pictures of the things around you. Let your imagination convince you that what you are seeing right now is in fact a painting. (It is not real, but it is just an image.) Then, when you feel quite comfortable with this image, switch back to your straightforward perception of your surroundings. Look around you and feel the actual presence of the objects around you. (They are not just an image;

they are real.) After half a minute or so, again imagine that this is all a painting. Play with this transition for a few minutes.

2.2

Now, redo the same exercise at 2.1, but this time by setting aside what is said in the parentheses. Stop interpreting your experience as one being more real than the other and instead let the things appear to you *as perceived* and *as imagined*. And as you switch from one to the other, observe the different ways in which your surroundings appear to you. How are things given to you in your perception? And how does the appearance of the things change when you switch to your imagination of them as painted images? Do you feel different when you are perceiving and imagining? How so? Make some notes on your observations.

2.3

Once you have completed a few rounds of this second exercise, take a moment to ask yourself if your sense of reality has changed at all. Do you still feel that your perceptual experience is as real as ever compared to your imaginary experience? Or do you feel that it's better to say that your perceptual experience *appears* more real because of the way you can relate to those objects in your perception? Similarly, is your imaginary experience less real than your perceptual experience? Or is it better to say that because of the way we relate to the imaginary objects, our imaginary experience *appears* less real? Go back to your experience to see which of these descriptions better fit your sense of the experience.

Observations

The main purpose of this series of exercises was for you to discover an open self that is free from the ties to the so-called reality and to the story (or stories) of reality that we tell ourselves. Playing with our perception was a way to help you get a sense of this freedom. The very idea of playing with perception may have been puzzling at first, but hopefully after going through this series of exercises, you now feel that we can play with our perception just as much as we can play with our imagination.

In Exercise 2.1, you observed the way we typically understand our perception and imagination. That is, under normal circumstances, we take our perceived world to be "real" and our imagined world to be "less real." As you made the transition from one to the other, you may have noticed that you feel you are putting a lot of effort to maintain your imaginary painting, while no such effort is required in your perception. You may have felt this way because you feel that when you imagine your surroundings as a painting, you are trying to make it "unreal," whereas when you perceive your surroundings, you are simply seeing "the real." This exercise was meant to bring out this typical understanding of our perception and imagination.

Then, in Exercise 2.2, we set aside a powerful belief that colors our understanding of perception and imagination. This is the belief that perception is our window to the outside reality, whereas what we imagine is something in our heads and therefore, "less real." Once we set aside this belief, we can begin to let things appear just in the way they present themselves to us. We neither affirm nor deny that what we perceive is real and what we imagine is unreal. Rather, we suspend judgment on whether or not what we experience accords with something actual. We simply attend to our experience just in the way it appears to us. This move doesn't dissolve the distinction between perception and imagination, but instead, it allows us to appreciate their difference in light of how they appear to us. It is similar to appreciating a story. We suspend judgment about whether the story is fictional or non-fictional. We decide to not take a story less seriously just because it is fiction or more seriously because it is non-fiction. By putting aside these classifications, we can appreciate the story just in the way it is told.

It is surprising how much we can discover about our experiences once we attend to the way things appear to us. When you let the perceived objects appear to you, you may have observed that you have a sense that you could look at the other side of the table, say, if you were to change your position. And if you were to go and try to pick up the table, you would feel its weight in your hands. But in the case of the imagined painting, none of this would be possible. Instead, if you were to touch the edge of the table, you would feel the flat texture of the paint that evenly stretches out on the canvas. And when you come very close to the painting, you would be seeing more of the paint than the depicted object. Even without actually carrying out these actions, whenever we perceive or imagine, we have these various senses of how we could relate to the perceived or imagined object. These senses are an important part of what constitute our experiences of objects. In fact, "reality" would not be "reality" if it weren't for these meanings that we carve out in our experiences.

So how do these observations change, if at all, our sense of reality? This was the question we raised in Exercise 2.3. If you made similar kinds of observations as above, you would most likely say that it is *not* that our perceptual experience is "more real" than the imaginary experience. Rather, it *appears* "more real" because our perception allows us to do things with our experience that imagination doesn't. It gives us the possibility to pick up objects and touch them, move around them, ask others to do the same, etc., which are all important for what we take to be "real." Likewise, it is *not* that our imaginary experience is "less real" than perceptual experience. It *appears* "less real" because it doesn't have the same characteristics as our perceptual experiences. But imagination allows us to do other things that perception doesn't, like making something be present that is not actually there. Indeed, this is exactly what you were doing when you imagined the painting of your surroundings. It was only because you believed that perceptual experience is "more real" that you thought that imagining the painting was a way of making your surrounding less present and therefore "less real." And that belief, which is a well-made story, was based on habit and convention, not on what actually appears to you in your experience.

But we should be careful with what we mean by "appearance" here. Oftentimes we use this word in contrast to objective reality. So, we would say, "He *appears* to be a nice person but *in reality* he's heartless." This is *not* the way we are using the word "appearance" here. We are not saying that perceptual experience subjectively appears more real when in reality or objectively it is something else. When we say that perceptual experience presents things as real, this is not a "mere appearance" of things, but the way in which things genuinely present themselves in perception. In attending to the appearance of things, we are not studying the surface level of things, but we are actually delving deeper into our experience by studying the various ways in which things appear to us in our experience.

Now, once you have recognized that your perception and your imagination are just different ways in which things appear to you in your experience, we can also recognize that we are not tied down to "reality" as much as we may have initially believed. For "reality" is not some established thing which we must obey, but rather, it is a specific way in which we apprehend the appearance of things. Reality is a story we tell ourselves.

You may have also noticed that this specific perspective that we have come to adopt is effectively the phenomenological perspective that Husserl and others established. What we therefore discovered, as a result of setting aside our belief that there is one "reality" which is offered by perception, is the realm of *phenomena*, namely the appearance of things in our experience. And as the one who observes the various ways in which things appear, we are neither the actual self that gets caught up in "reality" nor the imaginary self that momentarily escapes from it. Instead, we are the *phenomenological self* or the *open self* that has gained a bit more freedom by realizing that the sense of what is real (as well as what is imaginary) issues, not from some "outside reality," but from ourselves.[1] We are the storytellers of our reality.

Exercise 3: Playing With the Subject-Object Reversal[2]

In this last series of exercises, let's see if we can find a whole new dimension of openness and freedom as well as playfulness by letting phenomena play you, rather than you playing with phenomena.

3.1

Take an object that is in your visual perception. Carefully observe the object—its shape, size, color, etc. Then carefully observe *your experience* of the object. Your experience doesn't itself have shape, size, color, etc., but your experience grasps the object as having shape, size, color, etc. So, when you observe your experience of the object, your observation will look something like this: "I am looking at the ring that is round, small and silver." Note that your experience has a subject-object structure. "I" am the subject of the experience who is looking at the object, "the ring" in this case. Observe the way you feel the object being "over there," separate from you.

Now, reverse this subject-object relation. *Let the object look at you.* This doesn't mean you look at yourself "from the outside," so to speak, if you were to perform a meta-cognition of yourself. That would be to take up the place of the subject again, just a higher-order one. Rather, we are giving up the role of the subject altogether. You are no longer the subject of your experience. *Simply become the object.* In Japanese, the word for "object" (*kyaku* 客) means *guest* and "subject" (*shu* 主) *host*. Follow this image and let yourself be the guest. You're no longer the host, looking after your guests and making sure everything is in order. Let go of any control and just be a good guest by making yourself comfortable and enjoying what is offered to you. Let the host take care of you. Observe how your experience has changed after reversing the roles and taking up the role of a guest.

You might find it easier to do this with other people. Take a nearby person who is not looking back at you (s/he could be looking away or perhaps reading a book) and look at the person. You are the subject who is looking at the person, which is now the object of your perception. Now, ask the person to look at you while you look away. In doing so, feel the gaze of the other person. You may want to give the look back, but try resisting this temptation. Try to really give up your role as the subject and simply become the object of the other person's perception. Examine the difference between being the subject who objectifies the other and being the object of the perceiver. In what way do you feel they are different?

Once you have acquainted yourself with the subject-object reversal in this kind of interpersonal situation, go back to the above exercise with the object. Now that you have got a sense of what it is to be looked at by a person, see if it is easier to be "seen" by an object. If it's not easier for you, that is fine too. If you feel the two exercises are very different, observe the differences. In what way is it different?

3.2

Let us now do this same reversal for our other experiences. Instead of you thinking about what to have for dinner, let that thought think of you. Be a guest to the thought. This may be difficult because we like to think our thoughts are "ours," but try to see if you can let go of this grasping. Likewise, instead of you remembering your childhood, let your childhood memory remember you. Be a guest to the memory. And instead of you imagining that you are the unicorn, let that imagination imagine you. Be a guest to the imagination. If you're having a difficult time understanding what it could mean to "let the imagination imagine you" or "let the memory remember," don't worry. Allow the oddity and unnaturalness of these phrases to remain odd and unnatural. Reiterate these phrases in your head and see if your experience (not your intellect) would give you some hints. Try this reversal exercise for your other experiences. Let yourself become the guest to "your" experiences. Observe how your whole experience changes.

3.3

Now that you have played the role of both the host and the guest of your experience, practice reversing the roles for a few minutes. Let yourself be the host, and then become the guest. Try reversing roles for the same experience and see how you feel your experience change. Do this for your other experiences too.

After you have reversed a few times and feel comfortable playing both roles, see if you can be neither the host nor the guest, that is, neither the subject nor the object. See if you can just be the "stage" upon which the subject and object play their roles. Let the experience take place and simply witness this. You are no longer the subject looking at the object or the object being looked at. There is simply, "looking." Likewise, instead of you thinking about dinner or the thought of dinner thinking about you, there is simply "thinking" taking place. Going back to the host-guest metaphor, rather than being either the host or the guest, let yourself be the home that welcomes both. Stay with this experience for a while and observe how your experience has changed. Then ask yourself: *Where am I? Who is the one that is witnessing the subject-object play?*

Observations

The purpose of this series of exercises is to *really* open up to the appearance of things. While Exercise 2 can serve as a nice pathway towards this end, it also comes with a strong sense of subjectivity or agency. It opened us up to the appearance of things, but they were necessarily appearing *to you*. What's more, without your specific apprehension of the appearances, they didn't have the senses that they have. The purpose of Exercise 3 was to explore if we could go beyond this subjective take on appearances. Does the appearance of things necessarily have to be appearances for someone? Is "my" experience necessarily mine or is that just a result of my grasping the experience as mine?

In Exercise 3.1, we started by noting the way we usually attend to our experiences. Most of the time, when we reflect on our own experiences, we say: "I perceive X, I imagine Y, I remember Z, etc." Even when we don't articulate our experiences in this way (as when we're just vaguely attending to our experience or in the case of languages that don't necessarily have this kind of structure), we still have a sense that when I look at the ring on the table, "I" am looking at "the ring." In other words, there is a sense that "the ring" is over there and that "I" am somewhere over here. The sense of the "I" may not be very strong, but at the very least you are aware that the object is separate from you. We assume the subject-object duality to begin with, at least for the most part of our experience.

After bringing out this subject-object structure of our experience in our visual perception of looking at an object, we tried reversing the subject-object relation. Visual perception is a good place to start because it is relatively straightforward to reverse the relation compared to other kinds of experience. In fact, we do this all the time with people. We look at other people (i.e., you are the subject) and they look back at you (i.e., you become the object). But in interpersonal relationships, when we become aware that we are being looked at, there is usually a strong impulse to react. Whether it is by just giving the look back or by trying to impress the other, as soon as we are aware of others' gaze, we become very self-conscious. Perhaps with animals we have less of an impulse to react in this way, but we still become aware of ourselves as the subject. This is why we took an object as our first case instead of either another person or an animal. For although it might have been much easier to reverse the subject-object relation, it wouldn't have been easy to actually give up the role of the subject.

But even with objects, it still takes a lot of effort and patience to give up the role of the subject. Perhaps in the beginning it may not have made any sense to you. But after some practice, you may have noticed that letting go of control is a key factor. When we are the subject of our experience, as we usually are, we don't notice how much we are actually trying to control our experiences. But as we gradually move away from the seat of the subject, we begin to see how much effort we put into being the subject. Every time you move your eyes and try focusing on some aspect of the object, you can feel yourself *doing* this. In letting ourselves be the guest to the experience and in letting the object be in control instead, we can begin to feel more relaxed. By being the object, there is less doing on our part.

As we moved to Exercise 3.2 and tried this reversal with our other experiences, you may have found some experiences harder than others. Reversing the thought from you thinking about what to have for dinner to that thought thinking about you may have been quite difficult. Part of the difficulty is due to the fact that we are so used to thinking that thinking is something that we *do* and thoughts are something that we *have*, they belong to us. This is why it is so difficult to get our heads around what it means for a thought to think of you. But it is important to realize that the difficulty comes more from our habitual ways of interpreting our experiences and less from the nature of the experience itself.

Similarly, it may have been difficult to let the memory remember you since we're so accustomed to thinking that remembering is something we *do* and memory is something you *have*. In Japanese, there is an expression *omoidasareru* (思い出される being remembered) which is the passive voice of *omoidasu* (思い出す to remember). This expression is used when some memory spontaneously comes back to you rather than you deliberately bringing up the memory yourself.[3] Like those times when a smell instantaneously takes you back to your childhood days. Letting our memory remember you is similar to these kinds of experiences. In both cases, you are invited as a guest to your memory. You are not doing the remembering, but the memory remembers you.

In contrast, reversing the subject-object relation in our imaginary experience may not have been as difficult. And perhaps you may not even have felt so much difference when you reversed the relation. This is probably due to the spontaneous and playful nature of imagination. When you imagine that you are the unicorn, in the beginning you may feel that you are the one who is doing the imagining. But as soon as you start getting lost in your imagination, that feeling starts to diminish. Instead, the spontaneity and playfulness of imagination makes it feel less of something we do and more of something that is simply occurring on its own. When we set our imagination free, it seems to take on a life of its own that plays itself out. So, the subject-object reversal of imagination may feel less demanding than some of our other experiences because we are often guests to our imagination.

After we played around with exchanging subject-object roles for our various experiences, in Exercise 3.3 we tried to see if we could be neither the subject nor the object. Again, just as reversing the subject-object relation made little sense when we tried to understand what that means in our heads, being neither the subject nor the object makes very little sense if we stay at this level of understanding. But if we have experimented with our own experiences and really played around with exchanging the subject-object roles, it shouldn't have struck you as such an odd suggestion. Once we have realized that we can give up the role of the subject in our experience, it is not so hard to give up the role of the object either. As we exchange roles, we realize that these are exactly just that, namely *roles*. So, we can play the role of the subject as the host of our experience, or we can play the role of the object as the guest of the experience. Or alternatively, we can also just sit back and enjoy the play of reality. In doing so, our experience does not disappear into nothingness. On the contrary, we can begin to see much more of the dynamic *happening* of our experience and the interplay of the subject-object roles taking place. We can playfully take up the roles if we choose to do so, but in doing so we don't have to identify ourselves with them. This freedom from identification allows us to enjoy the spontaneity of life and feel at home with ourselves regardless of what "you do" and who "you are." By tapping into that spontaneity and playfulness of our experience, which is present not just in imagination but in all our experiences, we can begin to really appreciate the play of reality. *How free are we now?*

Discussion Questions

- In this chapter, we provided exercises to help you learn to be more aware of the structures in your experience and to play with them. Is there an exercise here that you particularly like? Which one, and why do you like it? What has it shown you about your experience that surprises you?
- The exercises in this chapter help you directly see in your own experience what we covered in a more theoretical manner in Chapter 3. After doing the exercises, go back to Chapter 3 and reread it. Do you feel your understanding has deepened about any specific points we discuss? Do you have new questions that came up after doing the exercises?
- All three exercises explore various dimensions of being more open, playful, and free. Compare the way you felt more open, playful, and free after doing each exercise. Do you feel these progressively expanded as you continued the exercises?

5

A Conversation with Contemplative Traditions

Philosophical activity involves two things: reflective distance and re-engagement. You need to distance yourself from practical involvements if you are to start reflecting on philosophical questions like "Who am I?" or "What is the meaning of all this?" But such distancing is only one side of what philosophy is about. Equally important is re-engaging with our practical lives in light of what we have learned from taking a distance with respect to them.

In general philosophers tend to emphasize distancing over re-engaging. We don't go to a philosopher today to seek practical advice on how to live. Edmund Husserl was no exception. He developed the method of suspending our basic belief in the existence of the world in order to study things purely in the way they present themselves to us. And ultimately, this was all towards the end of establishing a foundational science of all sciences. Husserl's phenomenology was very specific in its aim and it wasn't so much about enriching our practical lives.

But I believe philosophy can and should be about transforming the way we live based on the various insights gained through reflection. Philosophical reflection should be ultimately practiced towards the end of achieving a more truthful relationship with reality.

In this book, I reinterpreted phenomenology's central method, the phenomenological epoché, and complemented this with the practice of play. While the epoché is a reflective method of distancing ourselves from our beliefs and judgments, play is the practice of re-engaging with reality.

When we hear the word "play," we usually associate this with non-serious, light-hearted activity that has no purpose outside of itself. It is often accompanied with a sense that it is unimportant compared to the rest of the stuff we do in order to achieve this or that end. But in fact, there is nothing more important than playing with reality! I'm not suggesting we should manipulate reality into whatever you want it to be, as the phrase may suggest. Playing with reality in the specific sense here means letting reality speak from itself. We are dealing with a higher sense of play that requires lots of practice and discipline.[1] In this chapter, we'll see how my version of the epoché and the idea of playing with reality connects with some of the Asian contemplative traditions.

Steven (S) Thanks very much for the opportunity to discuss this, Yuko! I want to first comment on the double-sided point you just mentioned about philosophical activity involving reflective distance and re-engagement. In contemplative traditions like Buddhism, people are encouraged early on to train their awareness so it has some degree of reflective capacity and what you call "distance." Further training refines, focuses, and concentrates the awareness, enabling real insight. Meaningful engagement and further learning follow naturally. This balanced approach is challenging for people, because they may misunderstand it as isolationist withdrawal, or want to rush past it to something more exciting . . . or remain at a "distance" rather than re-engaging. Your statement protects against imbalanced approaches.

Yuko (Y) So we already see an important parallel. Looks like we're off to a good start!

S Interestingly, your presentation of phenomenology shows that re-engagement itself further informs and refines the understanding gained through the reflective distance. And this is also the view in contemplative traditions—life is contemplation in action and even active contemplation, not just the application of contemplative insight gained via distance.

Y I very much like that: contemplation in action or active contemplation. You could say that what I am introducing in this book is *phenomenology in action* or *active phenomenology*. But we have to be careful here. I'm not saying that phenomenology as it was introduced by Edmund Husserl in the beginning of the last century (or any of its later developments) has this character. As I said earlier, Husserl's phenomenology was very specific in its aim and it wasn't so much about enriching our practical lives.[2]

So when I say phenomenology in action or active phenomenology, I'm already taking phenomenology beyond what philosophers understand by it today. Most importantly, whereas Husserl emphasized distancing over re-engaging, I emphasize the inseparability of the two approaches.

S You just mentioned that Husserl's emphasis was not on enriching our practical lives. I do recall him writing on ethics and value theory. Do you feel even that work was literally more theoretical in its objectives than your own approach? This is important to me because ethics, for example, plays a major and very concretely lived role in traditional contemplative practice.

Y Indeed, Husserl wrote quite extensively on ethics, though that part of his philosophy is perhaps less acknowledged. In fact, he even says that phenomenology is not only about providing a foundation for knowledge, but also for ethical values.[3] He even speaks of the epoché at some point as a method that demands a personal transformation and compares it to a religious conversion.[4] This kind of statement and his general interest in ethics suggest that the aim of Husserl's phenomenology wasn't just theoretical but also practical. This is a controversial point that I would prefer to leave for Husserl scholars to debate.

S Thanks. So coming back to your interpretation of phenomenology, how do you see phenomenology connecting with contemplative traditions?

Y In this book, I introduced the epoché, or suspension of judgment, as a useful tool to play with reality. And as I said, this idea was borrowed from phenomenology. But in classical phenomenology, you don't really find this method put to use in the way we have been doing here. First of all, the context is different. The Husserlian epoché was introduced within a very specific philosophical project. Here, we are presenting the epoché as a practical tool for anyone curious enough to explore the nature of reality. Second, we have stretched the sense of the epoché from suspending judgment on the world (its existential status and the various meanings it has for us) to suspending judgment on the subject-object split that pervades much of our way of relating to the world. This last bit reflects my own interest in Japanese philosophy and specifically in Nishida Kitarō's philosophy. More specifically, since Nishida was trained in Zen Buddhism, it reflects the Zen Buddhist insight that true reality is beyond the subject-object duality. This allows us to naturally ask how the ideas presented in this book resonate with some of the views of the contemplative traditions.

S I'll begin by talking about the subject-object split you just mentioned. This topic provides us with a simple way of introducing several primary points in contemplative traditions, and we can then see how they relate to your presentation on phenomenology.

Y Let's try it.

S OK. In any ordinary discussion where someone is talking about going beyond the subject-object split, I would have to acknowledge that for many people this would seem to be a strange idea. And in fact it could mean a number of different things.

Y That's a really good point. When we talk about the subject-object duality in philosophy, we often assume this means the epistemological distinction between the knower and the known. Nishida was operating with this meaning for the most part. But I think that he also meant several different things with this.

S I'd like to explain the different ways it's understood in a few contemplative traditions that I've studied and teach. So rather than thinking of the subject-object split as one thing, I'll just take it as a range of related things, drawn from these traditions. This could be a way of giving our readers some examples of what dealing with this "split" might look like.

Y Where should we start?

S People are different, so in a one-on-one teaching context that would be a personal and pragmatic question. But for general expository purposes, I find the easiest place to start is with the Confucian tradition . . . It basically agrees that for most people there is a kind of disconnected sense of self that should be corrected, allowed to mature further. The typical, limited version of the self cuts us off from other people and also from the mature form of our own humanity. Confucianists consider it an immature form of personhood and call it the "small self." There's a Mandarin written character for this.

Y I believe this is "小我," literally "small self."

S That's right, thanks! The Confucian view is that people start out with the small, separate self. And unfortunately this same form of self is generally retained for far too long . . . a "little kid" holdover. Someone could be 55 years old and still be a little kid in this sense. So we need to make a real effort to grow up . . . to become a mature or "true" human being. And that means maturing into being a "self for others"—represented by another Mandarin character.

Y Is this "大我," literally "greater self"?

S Well, I was specifically thinking of 仁 here, Ren, a "self with others" rather than an isolated self. And the Confucian meaning of "self for others" pushes the point even further. So I'm claiming the Confusion analogue to Nishida's idea is to recommend a maturation process and form of learning. You let go of the self that separates itself off from other things and people, and discover, through a focused form of learning and living, a self that's connected to all situations and people. Especially to people, and to their needs as human beings. You become more deeply connected to everyone as fellow human beings.

Y This reminds me of the example of my friend who had the realization that she wasn't trying to listen to him, but only hearing what she wanted to hear. In your words, she saw that the small self was separating itself from the situation and her partner.

S Yes, her small self was doing that, inevitably. And probably so was his. Here we become involved in the great undertaking of trying to bring people together, growing up to participating in the true human community. This requires intimate co-presence. It's a matter of overcoming separation on every level . . . finding a basis of caring for others, and eventually even a true sense of participation on community and social levels. It sounds like a pretty simple view, but I think it's quite challenging and profound to really do it, live it.

Y It seems to me that reconnecting to the true human community is an enormous task that is several steps ahead of reconnecting to another human being or to one given situation. It's hard enough to get rid of the separation to one human being, how can we bring all people together? Where do we even begin?

S As you know, traditionally it would start when we're children, within the family. But nowadays, I guess we must start where we can. Wherever it seems possible. It's pretty easy to describe the basic steps. Just look into how you are currently *not* doing it—sincerely and diligently investigate that. This amounts to caring about the issue, at least a little bit, from the beginning. Sincerity, diligent investigation, and caring are key terms for the Confucian approach. Even a little bit leads to more, based on caring enough to assess and investigate.

Y Starting off with the question, "how am I not doing it?" is much more helpful than simply saying let's reconnect. If you don't know what is hindering you from truly caring for other people, you wouldn't know how to go forward. It's very important to know your habits.

S Exactly! Basically what people in this tradition did was to systematically ask themselves "How did I do today? Did I push people away from me or disconnect from them and their needs, while being caught up in my own small preoccupations? Or did I stay connected with people and try to respond in a way that served the purposes—really the true needs—of everyone present?"

This simple-sounding Confucian-style practice is not precisely a phenomenology practice, but they have points in common. It's certainly a contemplative practice in the classical sense. Nothing exotic ... just contemplation using ordinary thought and reflection. You sit down at the end of the day, and consider how your day went. You remember what happened, and if you're honest and sincere, you may decide that at times you were acting in a "separate self" sort of way. You see that it happened in one or more particular situations, and you examine what specifically triggered it. You can learn that such cases push you in the wrong direction, so you decide to watch out for those, try to handle them better. You can also aspire to be more like other people you know, mentors or exemplars of some sort, who seem to be more considerate of other people and sensitive to the real demands of a given situation. This requires learning, trial and error.

Y This method indeed has a lot in common with the phenomenological practice. One similarity I can see immediately is that both emphasize the importance of direct observation. You look at your own experience to see what is happening in a given situation and extract the patterns across the various experiences. Perhaps one obvious difference is that in classical phenomenology, the phenomenological attitude doesn't necessarily change the natural attitude, our default way of relating to the world. Of course, the phenomenological practice I presented in this book is very different from the classical view in this regard. It is much more in line with the contemplative practice since we are ultimately aiming to transform our ordinary way of relating to ourselves, to others and to the world.

S That distinction is crucial. And in order for this transformation to succeed, it must be "practiced," repeated on a regular basis. For example, each day reserve a couple of minutes to reflect on what happened in your actions and responses. Here we have a practice based on remembering—using our memories of things that occurred. But it's also based on a commitment to improve. You must make a commitment to try to do better in your interactions. For example, commit to waiting an extra few seconds or minute to see what other people are saying to you. What's really going on with them, what would be useful to them in that situation? Commit to taking more of that in, rather than just ignoring it and narrow-focusing on your own ideas and agendas—the agendas of a disconnected self. This is only a very small part of what a real

Confucian sense of maturation would involve, but it's important in its own right and sufficient for our present purposes.

During the evening of the next day, you again reflect . . . how did that day go? Did you follow through on your commitment or did you just forget the whole thing, or get taken over by some habit . . . you review how your commitments related to your actual behavior. You just reflect, learn, and try your best, from day to day.

Initially here you're just looking for something that's an improvement on limitations you've noticed. You're dealing with a self that's the instigator of actions based on a separateness that's pretty obvious if you're willing to look. And you're stating your new objectives, which emphasize cultivating more connection, caring, and commitment to acting on behalf of all. That's the main theme, trying to learn what that truly means, initially through a regular practice of reflection on what typically happens and what might be better.

Y I can see how such practice could already bring so much change. It seems simple and easy to do but taking some time to reflect and take note of the practice everyday is already something quite challenging to do. It's a real commitment.

S This might seem hard, but we're talking about living up to our natures and opportunities to have the best lives we can, together. It's worth the trouble. As you actually carry this investigation further, what you notice is that occasionally you get past the artifice of the practice, the structured discipline of working through your memories of the day and making commitments for the next day. Let's face it, all practices are somewhat artificial, and contemplative traditions admit that. Also, this practice involves a certain degree of idealism. But eventually you will move beyond the artifice and idealism, and instead find a natural and more direct connection to the essence of what's really important. And this is always a surprise. You can't and shouldn't try to anticipate such a thing. It's just natural—uncontrived, new, and unfamiliar but still recognizably "you" in some important sense. It's not just an artifact of a method, it's closer to the real "you" and you're—naturally—happy to be that.

Y This is an important point that connects directly with the epoché practice. Learning to play with reality is not like learning to do something completely new. Playing with reality is something that is originally natural for us. We were doing it all the time when we were children. But as we grow up, we get more and more separated from reality by creating various sorts of barriers. These barriers can occasionally break down spontaneously as we saw in some of the examples of falling into the play of reality in Chapter 2. But we can also practice trying to set them aside intentionally. This kind of practice is a way to re-learn how to play with reality. At first it feels unnatural for us since it is more natural for us to see with our colored glasses we have become so accustomed to. But eventually we can begin to enjoy playing with reality as it gets more and more natural for us. Playing with reality is something so close to us yet it is also something that is forgotten most of the time.

S In its stereotypical forms, Confucianism can seem very sober or solemn. But even Confucius himself described an emphasis on learning each day, and ultimately realizing—making real—a naturally relaxed, free way of being. So here I'm just saying we start with reflecting and experimenting in this somewhat disciplined way, and thus discover or make explicit contact with tendencies and habits of mind that diminish true caring and acting for others. I think these limiting habits are closely related to what you're encouraging people to notice and suspend via the epoché. The idea in both cases is to see these tendencies clearly, and move past them.

Your nature surfaces and declares something like "I actually do care, I'm connected to everyone present and would act on their behalf." Moreover, this kind of action is spontaneous. So the approach is initially structured, perhaps even a bit strict, but the result is very free, spontaneously responsive. Thus, while Confucianism seems rigid, it's really about finding and exercising free and apt responsiveness in the context of all human interactions.

Y Very interesting. The epoché too is more of a structured practice that requires much discipline which is not always fun. But the result, playing with reality, is fun and definitely liberating.

S A common ground is there, then. Good! Moving on to the Daoist approach, the counterpart to the issue of disconnection here is the disconnect from your own aliveness. And the disconnect from the living world that is continuous with the aliveness within you. What is within and around you are continuous, not separate. You are alive and that aliveness is inseparable from the living world and Nature. They're all facets of one presence. So what you're concerned with here is a little different from the focus in the Confucian tradition. Instead of bringing out what the Confucianists would call "true humanity" or "human-heartedness," you're bringing out this aliveness. You're participating in it more, and based on it more.

Y That is a nice way to contrast the two approaches. "Human-heartedness" is part of our aliveness but this aliveness is also much more expansive than that. Humans are just a small part of a bigger living nature.

S In this Daoist view, the small self is the self that ignores that vast, multi-dimensional context of aliveness. A better alternative is one that doesn't ignore or go against what your aliveness wants, but the small self is always making that perverse mistake to some degree. It's ignoring the living world, oblivious to it because of small-mindedness and because of a contracted posture or existential stance. The alternative is one of acknowledging our connection to aliveness within and without, based on the promptings of our nature's intelligence, its attunement. This is not a fantasy. It's very real, palpable. Living from it is quite doable and important, just as living from more of our true humanity, humaneness, is very important.

Y I feel it has become more and more hard for us to acknowledge this aliveness both within and without. We believe we are in control of our lives as well as of other living beings. And we forget how vast aliveness really is.

S Yes, isn't that strange? Gradually, on both the social level and as individuals, we've slid into ignoring it. The shift back, the "return," is one that some people understood and explicitly cultivated in the past, and we can also make it now. It's just a matter of noticing both the issue and what goes against it, then seeing and feeling which is better. That takes some training, hence the need for practice. One simple training exercise, which I often like to teach and is derived from the classic *Dao De Ching* text, is to practice not going to the limit.

Don't go to the limit in anything, stop a bit short of it. Because we're disconnected from our body–energy–mind living nature, and from what's speaking to us in the living world around us, so we go too far, in many aspects of life. We're rather excessive creatures in that way, and can benefit from some re-tuning.

Y We sure are. Our smartphones are constantly feeding us with updates from friends to news around the world. We can't go anywhere without our phones and we fall asleep with it in our hands.

S I hope that trend moderates. People's living nature is vastly more important—and interesting, meaning, and satisfying—than any phone could be. Even the food we see in the grocery store can communicate more to us more than we usually realize. In comic book terms, it's saying "don't eat me, I'm not right for you at the moment" or "do eat me, I'm what you need." There's a rich connection to each item but we're usually oblivious of this. The sense of self we've acquired is what gets in the way. Just like in the Confucian case—

there's a small self that's missing this connection and because this self is constantly saying "I want to live from habits, and I want to fix my sense of dissatisfaction, of being incomplete," it's always heedlessly chasing and grasping at one thing, then later at others to counter the dissatisfying consequences of the earlier grasping. On and on it goes, using up life.

Y This all sounds very familiar. Rather than trying to listen to your own mind–body, we do what habit tells us to do. And this habit is socially and culturally cultivated, which makes it even more difficult to counteract. You mentioned the grocery store—well, unless you are very careful, too often we end up buying things we don't really need. Things are always calling out "Take me! Take me!"

S Right! Living in a disconnected way causes us to grasp at things to fill a perceived lack. It also makes true fulfillment impossible. The small, disconnected self is always chasing and grasping, and in the process, it's going way past the limits of what our basic living nature wants, needs, or can properly do. It makes us chase around even when we're very tired and need to rest. These basic, common-sense points, obvious but seldom taken to heart, are actually considered quite profound in Daoism. "The wise seem like fools."

Y It might be common sense but all of us need to be reminded of this quite seriously. I think we often don't realize how much we are actually going beyond what our basic living nature needs. We are unaware of this fact. I have to remind myself all the time.

S We all do. So the simple exercise of correcting that grasping/chasing run-on tendency could be very important. Go to bed before you get too tired. Don't wait until you're exhausted, do it when you still have a little energy . . . sleeping properly actually requires energy. The same point applies with eating. Or talking with people. Or watching a movie or roving around the internet. Or listening to music. Enjoy things, but stay in a middle territory. Your living nature is tracking our activities and our habitual straying into excess, and knows when it's time to stop or to do something else—to make a different connection or tap into a different source of inspiration. Don't go to the limit, stop short of it. Make a commitment to that effect, and gradually learn to hear your nature's promptings.

Y This I think may be extremely difficult for many of us to do. There is so much to do and so much to choose from. We have access to so much information by simply turning on our phones. If we put a limit to this, we would be missing out on so much. Or at least this is the way most of us think nowadays.

S It could become an endless unchecked and heedless drift. So in this practice, as with the Confucian case, you sit down at the end of the day and reflect on how the exercise went. What really happened that day? Usually the answer will be that in many respects, you still went to the limit or even past it. And you can gradually learn to see the consequences of having done so. Don't be upset about "failing," or feel guilty. Just honestly document the instances, the different kinds of cases, where you went too far. And yes, note the consequences. This helps re-educate or stimulate our natural capacity for feeling and understanding what's happening in life.

Y I can say from my own experience that taking this time to reflect and observe is extremely important. I often find myself feeling very tired at the end of the day without knowing why. Only upon reflection do I realize that this is because I had been spending so much time looking at the screen in the same position. If I hadn't taken the time to stop and reflect, I would keep on doing the same thing and keep on being tired. Simply reflecting on this won't immediately change what I do, but it will make me more aware of what is happening and what is required to bring out the change. Reflecting allows you to stop in your tracks.

S Initially, because of the power of our habits, you won't be able to tell what a "limit" is, but you can at least sense that you don't feel right in some way. Start with noticing that, even if it's still not very clear. Gradually you'll get better at discerning what really happened and exactly how it affects you. Limits become more concretely sensed too. You can track your living nature's condition and reactions better. Until that happens, just notice that you must have gone too far somehow, look into that, and document as much as you can. "What did I actually do, why, for how long, in what situation, with what consequences?" Then you try again the next day to keep your commitment to stop short of your limits in various senses, and again document the results. I think if someone tried this even for two weeks, it could make a big difference in the quality of life.

Y Yes, if we really commit ourselves to this, I can definitely see how this would bring so much change in both our awareness and our way of being.

S Gradually your awareness will increase and you'll stay in a more healthy middle territory, partly because of discipline, partly because the exercise is still artificial and forces us to do things a certain way, but also because you're learning to stay more in touch with your nature. This latter part is the surprise factor, again, like in the Confucian case. You tap into an inner guide. So in this rather simple way, you're overcoming a disconnect related to the separation issue that Nishida discusses, coming more from his Zen Buddhist training.

What I'm currently describing is not Zen Buddhism, just a very elementary Daoist analogue. Even so, the result is somewhat similar: there is no longer an attachment to a separate self. The being that you truly are is part of an overall context of being, there is less of an entrenched separation. This probably won't be a sudden or shocking awakening, such as is sometimes considered to be part of the Zen tradition's path. It's an easily accessible insight of a related kind, that I think would be very helpful to anyone. By comparison, Nishida's insight and the Zen realization that stand behind it can be quite difficult for many people to understand. I'm just offering examples of simpler practices and insights that may naturally tie into the phenomenological investigations you have described, Yuko. And that also might serve as a bridge to Nishida's understanding.

Y Indeed this is very helpful. "Going beyond the subject-object split" sounds very abstract and perhaps even mystical, but talking about reconnecting with our living nature is something we can all relate to in one way or another. And this fits very well with what we have been discussing in this book too. In Chapter 2, I mentioned my experience of falling into the play of nature when I saw "the dancing leaves." There was a clear perspectival shift that happened then. It was the same tree with its leaves, but I was seeing something different. It was not there anymore as something that creates a nice shade for me. I was rather simply witnessing the dancing leaves, the beautiful play of nature. It was such a liberating moment where my usual way of perceiving nature had been replaced by a much more intimate connection with it. And this came with the realization that this connection had been there all along, but I had somehow lost sight of it.

These insightful moments can be helpful in pointing us to what we have forgotten. But the most important thing is to make a commitment not to forget. We can only do this by introducing some sort of discipline. The practice that you have just suggested is a wonderful way to remind ourselves that we human beings are also a part of the play of nature.

S Right. And in addition, perhaps based on that grounded sense, there are still more opportunities for seeing and appreciating life. To give another example, I could mention the general kind of contemplative training common to most schools of Buddhism. Not all Buddhist teaching is at the Zen level, but I think it all does concern the sense of being a self. The historical Buddha made rather subtle comments to the effect that the self is not what we think it is, and that this "self" introduces some problems. Buddhists accept that the self exists in some senses, but the tradition still recommends investigating precisely in what respect and to what extent there is a "self." Seeing more of what is really involved in the apparent self is the issue. It's not everything we assume it to be, it's actually not the center of everything in life. The self's views, preferences, values, and reactions are not really as important, or as valid, as we think. The self is also not a continuous and permanent thing nor a solid substantial thing. It's not the owner of perception or the thinker of thoughts, as is also taken for granted. But to see these points clearly takes a lot of "meditation" training or perhaps something like the discipline of the epoché you've been explaining here. So for the purposes of our present chat, just to make things very simple, I'll give two introductory practices to supplement what you've already introduced.

Y Dismantling this false sense of the self is quite a daunting task. This seems to me part of the reason why Buddhist practice strikes us as something that only the committed few are capable of doing. So I'm eager to hear what kind of introductory practices you will give us.

S The first is to moderate the "scattered, separate, reactive, grasping, chasing self" a bit. Practice settling down. Such practice is basically common to most all contemplative traditions. Settle, stabilize, and focus a bit, connect to the body and breath. Trying this on a daily basis would be a big help. A hard, sharp, narrow-focus is not necessary for our present purpose, just a general "being present, seeking nothing beyond the simplicity of this" is enough. The self-asserting pattern of mind and feeling is not comfortable with such simple presence. Boredom, heightened reactivity, fidgeting will follow. That's because the self-obsessed viewpoint doesn't accept that what we are in a more fundamental, direct, and natural way, is sufficient. The small self is really at best a limited stance, and often a misleading one. So here our practice is just countering the self's mistaken views for a little while. Technically this is called "calm abiding," but the traditional form of that method already brings in more complexity than we need for our present discussion. The reader can just try settling down a bit.

Y This practice is extremely important and relevant for the purposes of this book. All the practices that I introduced in Chapter 4 assume that you are already settled down to some extent and ready to play along. But many of us are in fact not prepared. So many things are going on in our lives with so many distractions. Our attention is scattered. That is why we have to first practice to settle down, stabilize, and focus, as you say. This prepares our mind and body to do any kind of contemplative practice, including the phenomenological practices introduced in the last chapter.

S OK, good. Then the only complication I'll introduce here is to add that settling down doesn't mean being a "calm self"—that's not necessary or relevant. The point is to find a calm acceptance of a few minutes of life whether the self is calm or not! Setting up a calm self would just be more grasping for conditions and affects of the self. Notice whether you're calm or not, that much could be useful information! But whether the self is calm or restless, even agitated, embrace another sort of calmness available within your nature, a fundamental accepting resource that's seldom noticed but could be a great support throughout our lives. Why disconnect from that? It only happens because we get tricked by subtle tendencies and habits, and these can be reversed.

Y When we start any kind of meditation practice, we tend to think we have to be calm. And when we are not calm, we get discouraged that the practice is not working. But as you say, that is not the point. We can simply start by following the rhythm of the breath and simply focusing on that. As your attention becomes more and more focused on the breath, we discover a stillness that comes with a specific kind of clarity.

S Yes, exactly! And going further, I could suggest a second practice, based on the first. This might involve an explicit commitment to a kind of natural ethics. For instance, take up a particular precept of conduct for a while—like "don't harm," "don't steal," or "don't lie." Pick one of these, and try to make a daily experiment of holding it throughout the day. As with our previous exercises, review the results at the end of each day, see what happened, and why and with what consequences. Decide how to improve your approach for the next day, and continue.

Y This practice is similar to the "don't go to your limits" practice, but also quite different. It may take time to start noticing what our limits are before we can stop short of our limits. But with "don't harm," "don't steal," or "don't lie," it seems straightforward enough to put it into practice right away.

S Yes, it might take a while to see the connection, but both are concerned with an errant or excessive tendency. Using guiding precepts or rules might seem artificial, not very natural. And probably it seems very basic, trivial, or convention-bound. But that's how all practice starts, partly because that's where our ordinary mind is, at the outset. The point is to encourage further learning and discovery. Conditioning factors that compromise our actions in life, and fundamental—natural—values that guide and enrich life, can gradually be seen.

Y Right. So initially, we might be simply following one of these precepts just because it is the right thing to do. Like "don't harm," we all know it's wrong to harm others. It's so basic and obvious. But then, as we make it into a practice to follow this sincerely, we start to see that this basic precept may not be as obvious as it seemed.

S Many generations of traditional contemplatives have found that to be so. Proceeding in this way, our understanding of the real meaning of a precept like "don't lie" can undergo a vast reconsideration and transformation, based on seeing more clearly. Things that initially don't seem like harming, lying, or stealing may gradually be sensed to still be violations of the precept, perhaps on more subtle or "inner" levels . . . so you learn and adjust to a new version or understanding of the precept, and continue.

Y And such reconsideration and transformation would only happen if we commit ourselves to really practicing this in our daily life and taking time every day to reflect and observe how we have been doing.

S I don't want to scare people off, but yes, some degree of commitment is necessary. Then such practice will again show how the separate, habit-bound, and reactive sense of self involves limited and limiting beliefs and assumptions rather than actual reality. Don't harm or take from others, foolishly imagining that could somehow help your self. Don't fabricate reality, that just separates you from it, which is disabling . . . just as Daoism also says.

In traditional Buddhist practice, there are a lot of such precepts. Here I'm just suggesting picking one and working with it for a while, assessing results at the end of each day. The overall process is very similar to what I suggested for the other two traditions. As you see more, you become more committed to the exploration and that involves a stronger intention and exertion, more vigorous application.

Y Yes, I can now see how this practice is also very similar to the others. In this last practice, it may seem like we are just taking up basic rules and following them. But the point is not to blindly follow pre-given rules. Instead, the point is to make it your practice to try understanding the true import of the precepts. This involves, like all other practices you have introduced so far, commitment to practice everyday, including the time to stop and reflect on your practice.

S And you can also use the calm presence and other things we've discussed as supports for that vigor. The things that make us break our ethics precept include agitation and distraction, subtle discomfort . . . even distraction from our living nature and our humane connection to others. Because we're "out of sorts" in some way, we ignore or fail to perceive larger issues, the wholeness and truth of things, which are what the ethics precepts represent. When we're uncomfortable, we contract and then start serving narrower agendas, maybe without even noticing it.

Y Every time this "smaller self" comes up, we can note the instances, see how it prevented me from following the precept and what happened as a result. Keeping track of our failures is also an important part of this practice.

S Exactly! I always tell my students that, it's a primary point, in my opinion. Somewhat like in science, things that don't work out as expected are considered to be very instructive. So, based solely on our own discoveries, working with more awareness over time, we can put these pieces together and gradually find higher and higher levels of what the precepts really are—they're not just rules shoved at little kids to keep them in line, they show how we typically are lying to ourselves, stealing from ourselves, harming ourselves, as well as harming others and so on. How? We undermine our health, as the Daoists observe, or undermine other aspects of existence here together, as already discussed. So you can find a natural interest in keeping the precepts, a kind of higher insight-based interest—you just want to! Or even more precisely, you just do! It's in accord with an emerging sense of reality. Normally we don't have a sense of reality, only passively acquired beliefs—as you've discussed, Yuko—plus a sense of situations, recent local conditions, and things that serve the self's narrow purposes.

Y So we act in accordance with rules not because they are imposed on us from without, but because they express our fundamental and natural way of relating to reality.

S That's the primary reason. Anything else is at best just a temporary guideline. So, based on this emerging sense of reality, which can be somewhat glimpsed given these several simple practices, we can at least touch on the reality that concerns traditional schools such as Ch'an or Zen. I guess this is where Nishida's philosophy comes in, through his background with Zen. Zen is of course part of Buddhism, but at least for some of its practitioners it focuses on a level of awareness that's particularly advanced, well beyond what our chat and this book can really explain. Even so, the insight that the self is not what we generally assume is related to the Zen realization.

Y Nishida's philosophy is often criticized for being too mystical, coming from his extraordinary experience in Zen. It is true that an important part of his philosophy is based on insights from his own practice in *zazen*, which may not be easily accessible for people who are outside the tradition. But it's a mistake to say that therefore his ideas are only relatable to those few people. There is much in his philosophy that we can all relate to. As you say, the basic insight is that the "true self" is something other than what we normally think of as the self. There is nothing mystical about this idea.

S It's straightforward to see at least some of this point, it just takes investigation and also learning from daily life. In Zen and related schools of practice, the self is not only deconstructed in an analytic way, or partially dropped through exercises such as we've offered here which sharpen and ground our awareness. Instead, the self is fully released to an original ground or reality that can't be accessed through the ordinary mind. Really waking up. This is a totally fresh beginning, a fresh view. But it's related to the "surprises" I mentioned occurring in working with the simple Confucian, Daoist, and general Buddhist exercises. Just based on our own simple but sincere practice, including the phenomenological practices, we can embody this radically fresh view by staying as close as is possible to what is seen to be present. Present on an outer and also an inner level—what's happening around us and also within our own mind and feelings.

Y When Nishida was asked about various questions related to Zen, he often said "I don't know about Zen. Ask Suzuki Daisetsu." By referring people to Suzuki Daisetsu, who was his close friend from high school and also a serious Zen practitioner, he was acknowledging that the most important truths regarding the fundamental ground of our awareness and reality aren't something one can philosophically talk about. You just have to awaken to them. Nishida probably had some sort of direct insight into this, but he knew that Suzuki had gone deeper.

S We can all do something along those lines, it doesn't have to be extraordinary. Just step by step. There is a key point to Zen or other related schools of Buddhism that isn't "arrived at" at all, certainly not by a process of steps, but that gets beyond the scope of this presentation.

So to conclude, I could also comment on the topic of play, which you've emphasized. It might seem odd to link play to a program of exercises such as I've described. But I think an invitation to practice and learn is closely tied to the essence of play. Usually we're not aware of what we are, so we need to practice in order to recover that sense of ourselves and our reality. Then the practice aspect becomes less artificial and more natural, hence "playful." Play is a way of discovering and being fully yourself, what you really are, in a direct and complete, explicit engagement or integration with your context—the reality around you.

Y "Play is a way of discovering and being fully yourself. . ." That is nicely put. It takes a lot of practice to get there where we can naturally play again. But it's all worth it because it's so much fun and liberating to be able to play with reality!

S For Confucianism, you may start out practicing in a rather serious way, but the artifice flakes off and you end up with growing into your humanity, exercising it artfully and playfully—these are consistent with living responsibly. In Daoist practice the early training might again seem artificial, but in the end it's just being alive, in a space of aliveness. Manifest aliveness and then also more subtle forms of it. Full, free, spontaneous, creative exploration of that. And we can find a related thing in both general Buddhist training and in Zen, going beyond the limits introduced by attachment to an ordinary separate self . . . instead being what we truly are in the strictest sense. Play is experiential, exploratory, celebratory . . . and inseparable from reality, as you've said, Yuko.

Y "Celebratory" . . .! Somehow this word really captures the essence of play.

S Spontaneity and play seem very appealing, but it's actually difficult for most people to live based on those two things. It may take some practice! Based on practice, in the service of getting started, people can learn to be free of forms and rules. Not breaking them, but digesting their real import and appropriate application or expression.

So you don't go out and be spontaneous based on having read this book. Practice first, then find the basis for true play, in whatever way suits you personally.

Y It's important to be attracted to the idea of playing with reality, but this kind of playing isn't something that is easy to do. That is why I have focused on the practice of the epoché. Just as with the other practices offered in this chapter, if we commit ourselves to the various kinds of epoché practices, at some point we'll find ourselves naturally enjoying playing with reality. This form of play should be the outcome of all the practices.

S I'm sure the overall point of what you have described in this book would be very pleasing to the people engaged in these ancient traditions. They would recognize it as an encouragement to enter into an exploration that is wondrous. Practice supports learning, which leads to playful exploration, and eventually to wonder . . . living fully in the midst of wonder.

Y Wonder-ful! Thank you Steven for a great conversation. I think you have nicely illustrated how the ideas in this book relate to some of the ideas in the contemplative traditions.

Discussion Questions

- Consider how applying the epoché compares with the simple versions of traditional contemplative practices presented in Chapter 5. What similarities and differences do you notice? Can you see how both approaches involve a suspension of ordinary habits of the mind? What else do they involve?
- We've looked at some basic practices from the Confucian, Daoist, and Buddhist traditions. Which proposed contemplative practice would be most useful in your own life?
- We saw how "play" in the sense of "playing with reality" is not necessarily easy for us but instead requires much practice. This seems to contrast sharply with children's play, which is both natural and easy. Can you identify some other points of differences between the two senses of play?

Part Two

6

Practicing Phenomenology—the Historico-Theoretical Context

Steven (S) Yuko, in Part 1 you've presented enough on a new, streamlined form of the epoché to give people something to work with in daily life. And in Chapter 5 I made some basic comments on traditional contemplative regimens, to convey at least a sense of ancient traditional perspectives and types of practice as they might be applied nowadays. Hopefully those comments will also suggest how the traditions relate to the epoché. On that point, you've sprinkled some insights from Japanese culture and language throughout the book so far. I'd like to hear more. My teachers were Korean, Tibetan, and Chinese—none were from Japan. I can already sense there are some interesting differences that might deepen what we've introduced.

Yuko (Y) Yes, I do think that the Japanese background brings in some unique perspectives. It would be helpful to compare it with some of the traditions you mention to see what is particularly unique to the Japanese tradition.

S Before we go further in exploring particularly Japanese perspectives, let's summarize and develop the philosophy and phenomenology side more. That would probably help support those readers who would like to get a more in-depth explanation of the philosophical context of phenomenology and how it can be used … and how it might relate to both Japanese philosophy in the "Western" vein and to contemplative practice like Zen. Would you be willing to start by talking about practicing the epoché in more detail? Specifically, what did it mean in its early period, starting with Husserl, and continuing into the present?

Past, Present, and Potential Forms of Practice

Y Practicing phenomenology can mean a few things. I could distinguish three different meanings. One is what practicing phenomenology meant originally for the founder of phenomenology, Husserl himself.

Husserl's Understanding of Phenomenology

Y For Husserl, phenomenology was first and foremost a scientific method. "Scientific" in the sense that it is rigorous and systematic. It involved employing technical methods. Practicing phenomenology meant performing the phenomenological epoché and the reduction in order to clarify the essential structures of our experience. And this was tied to a broader philosophical project of providing a foundation for all other sciences.

At least in his later work, Husserl considered phenomenology to be a "transcendental" enterprise. There, he takes the idea of the transcendental from Kant, though it doesn't mean exactly the same thing. What Husserl understood by the term and how it differs from Kant's notion is a rather complicated matter. But, basically for Husserl, going transcendental means recognizing a kind of meaning-giving subjectivity at the ground of our experience without which the world would not have the meaning and validity it has for us.

So going transcendental for Husserl meant adopting a transcendental idealist position. This involves changing our normal way of understanding reality. When you become a transcendental idealist, you no longer believe that the world is out there existing separately from us. Rather, you understand that the world is constituted by the transcendental subject. It's quite a drastic change, which is why for Kant, it was called "Kant's Copernican Revolution."

S I can already see that the points you're raising here deserve some follow-up, to develop the issues involved. I'll defer that until you're done, then I'd like to come back with comments and questions for you.

Y Of course.

S One quick comment now though … in my own skimpy reading of Husserl, I noticed after the "later period" 1913 publication of his *Ideas*, Husserl's colleagues had a variety of objections to this "transcendental idealist" shift you mention.

Y Yes, I should say that Husserl wasn't always a transcendental philosopher. For example, his work in the *Logical Investigations*, published in 1900–1901, was not tied to any transcendental project although he was already doing phenomenology then. For the mature Husserl, however, phenomenology par excellence was transcendental phenomenology.

But you're right, that's the second case I was going to mention. Already in those days, some of Husserl's fellow phenomenologists rejected this transcendental turn.

Divergences from Husserl and Further Developments

For some of Husserl's colleagues, phenomenology was primarily about finding the essence of phenomena. Therefore, they were still doing what Husserl was doing, but separating it from the broader philosophical project of providing a foundation for all other sciences. You can say that they were still practicing phenomenology, though in Husserl's eyes this wasn't quite what phenomenology was all about. For these people, it didn't entail becoming a transcendental idealist. Doing phenomenology for them didn't involve changing our understanding of reality from the naïve realist view that says that the world is out there existing independently of us. Going transcendental is to undertake a kind of conversion. And this was too much to ask for most people. That's why there were quite a few who didn't accept Husserl's transcendental turn. These are the second type of phenomenologists, for whom practicing phenomenology meant a search for essences. They took up a part of Husserl's phenomenology while disregarding the broader philosophical project that Husserl had in mind.

The third sense in which one can speak of practicing phenomenology is situated outside of philosophy. Because phenomenology is essentially a methodology, a discipline that is not defined by its subject matter but its unique methodology, it can be used in various ways. And indeed, phenomenology has been practiced in psychology and psychiatry from early on.

Today, we also see it practiced in cognitive science, neuroscience, nursing, and also even biology. What they are doing is applying phenomenology in their specific fields for specific purposes. The way they apply phenomenology differs from discipline to discipline and even within a discipline it is often applied differently. And the exact way in which they are applying phenomenology is not always clear. But when people say they are adopting a phenomenological perspective, or applying phenomenology, they're usually taking the first-person point of view seriously. Sometimes, it involves much more than this, but often this is essentially what they are taking from phenomenology.

Many phenomenologists within philosophy would say that's not really enough to say they're doing phenomenology. And this may be true. But even then, they are taking up an important insight from phenomenology. In the sciences, the first-person perspective is usually identified with what is subjective and idiosyncratic and therefore non-objective and non-scientific. But phenomenology has shown that the first-person perspective can be taken up and investigated in a "scientific" way. Our lived experience is not merely idiosyncratic but has essential structures. When this insight is properly understood and applied in the sciences, phenomenology has made an important contribution.

So, we've got the original sense of practicing phenomenology in Husserl, which was tied to the transcendental project of providing the foundation for all other sciences. Then, we have the fellow phenomenologists for whom practicing phenomenology didn't mean taking up this grand philosophical project, but just extracting the essence of phenomena. And finally, I mentioned how one could practice phenomenology outside of philosophy. I'll also note the role of the epoché and reduction in these three groups.

How the Epoché Figures in Various Phenomenological Works

The phenomenological epoché and reduction are core methodological principles in phenomenology. Even for those who were not engaging in transcendental phenomenology but were only interested in finding the essence of phenomena, the epoché and reduction were part of what it meant to practice phenomenology. This is because doing phenomenological investigations requires temporarily setting aside the natural attitude and taking up the phenomenological attitude. And this involves bracketing our naïve belief in the existence of the world together with all the theories that are attached to this belief. Once we set aside this belief by performing the phenomenological epoché, we can then bring our gaze back to things just as they appear to us in our experience, which is what the reduction does as the meaning of the Latin word "reducere," to lead back, suggests.

But when people outside of philosophy adopt phenomenology, they are often not performing the epoché and the reduction. Dan Zahavi, a prominent Husserlian scholar and phenomenologist, has an interesting article titled "Applied phenomenology: why it is safe to ignore the epoché."[1] And there he argues that the epoché and reduction are not necessary for those disciplines that apply phenomenological method in qualitative research. Zahavi acknowledges that they are essential methods for Husserl and the philosophical enterprise he had envisioned, namely transcendental phenomenology. But precisely because of their technical nature, he argues that not only are they unnecessary but may even be harmful in that it creates a lot of confusion about what exactly the epoché and reduction are and how they are to be executed. His point is that qualitative research can make good use of phenomenological insights without getting involved with all the philosophical stuff. The latter are important for philosophical phenomenology only.

In academia today, you can find people practicing phenomenology in all of the three senses I mentioned, though probably not so much in the first sense. It's not so common to find people trying to do what Husserl originally envisioned with his transcendental program. Going transcendental is not so popular anymore. But also, the truth is that a lot of people who work in phenomenology don't really fit into any of these categories. They are scholars of phenomenology. What they're concerned with is exegesis.

So, these are Husserl scholars, Heidegger scholars, etc., mainly concerned with what Husserl and Heidegger really said in the texts and trying to get them right. And for such scholars, the practice aspect of phenomenology is completely lost. I won't say that's the majority of the people. But I do get the impression that a lot of people who say that they are phenomenologists, or that they work in phenomenology, are really only doing this kind of scholarly work. Which is not to say it is not important work. It is very important, but it's not quite the same as *practicing* phenomenology.

This Book's Approach to Phenomenological Practice and the Epoché

Y What we mean by practicing phenomenology in this book is not the same as Husserl's enterprise and it's also not the same as the second sense of what the early phenomenologist were doing, seeking the essence of phenomena. We ourselves haven't talked much about essences. One of the reductions is called "eidetic reduction." It's a core method for Husserl but I've avoided discussing that because it doesn't really contribute to our present purpose. So, it's certainly not the same as practicing phenomenology in the second sense. And we're also not applying phenomenological insights to some already established discipline.

The difference to Husserl's original version is that we're using the epoché for the purpose of improving our lives. Husserl speaks about the change of attitude, from the natural attitude, where you naïvely believe in the existence of the world, to a different kind of attitude, the phenomenological attitude, which is a rather unnatural attitude where you have suspended judgment about the existence of the world. But "change of attitude" sounds quite theoretical, some sort of mental operation one does like changing one's mindset.

To be sure, this change of mindset is quite radical since we're talking about setting aside a very basic attitude. But it doesn't involve changing one's *way of being*. When we talk about using the epoché to really make a difference in our lives, we're talking about a kind of *self-transformation*. It is about really changing the way you relate to reality and even changing your understanding of yourself. That's a huge difference to what Husserl originally had in mind with phenomenology.

For Husserl, the epoché had a narrow scope. It specifically meant bracketing our belief in the existence of the world. I agree with Zahavi that this is only relevant for phenomenology as a philosophical discipline. It's irrelevant for people working outside of philosophy. But instead of throwing it out altogether, what I've done is to take the epoché and reinterpret it to bracket not just our belief in the existence of the world, but any belief, really. In doing so, we've taken it out of the specific philosophical context it had when first introduced and put it into a practical context.

This means that practicing the epoché for us requires that we reflect on some of the closely held beliefs that we've acquired from our childhood, from our culture, upbringing, and so on. And then we bracket those beliefs so that they no longer color our perception of reality. I've interpreted the bracketing as a kind of *loosening of our grip*, which I think gets at the essence of what the epoché really does. First, we acknowledge that you have some belief, which can be about the world, but also about yourself, or about anything. And then you loosen your grip on that belief.

Loosening that grip may not seem to do anything on its own. But once you've loosened up, you have a different kind of relationship to your belief. You're no longer grasped by that belief. What you gain as a result is a bit more freedom, more space, more openness that allows you to further explore what the world has to offer. And this freedom or openness in turn allows you to start *playing with reality*. The goal of the practice is to play with reality. But this goal is a peculiar one in that there's no real end. It's an open-ended exploration. Playing with reality doesn't have a specific end where you can say, "Okay, that's it. I'm done." It requires a lot of practice to get a sense of what it may mean to play with reality. Further practice involves getting a deeper understanding of it and exploring its various dimensions. So, playing with reality is an ongoing exploration that never ends.

S Great summary, thanks Yuko!

Y I know that was a lot ... but I wanted to provide a bigger picture on phenomenology so that we can better situate the kind of "phenomenology" we are doing in this book.

Husserl's Philosophical Background—Kant's Innovations

S I noted many discussion points in what you just said. And recalling my own background as an undergraduate and graduate student in philosophy, I sense your comments about Kant, for instance, might be a good place to start because his work tends to confuse and even scare people ... like venturing into a deep dark forest. So, I'd like to expand on your first comments, tackling the notion of "transcendental philosophy" and related terms like "transcendental subject" vs "empirical subject" (or "ego"), and particularly "idealism" and "transcendental idealism." You can correct me when I get something wrong. I share your reluctance to say much about Kant's views in this sort of context, but I think a little bit would help us explore our main topic further. Is that OK?

Y Sure.

S All right, first—"idealism." The language issues here get tricky. Obviously in ordinary non-technical English it refers to optimal outcomes or maybe even "the ideal" or to "having ideals" where the emphasis is on what would be optimal, or on having high standards, upholding virtue, or even something spiritual. But in technical philosophical English, it concerns the centrality of ideas in a sense associated with Plato, or—going much further down the rabbit hole—a view of reality that emphasizes the mind, the domain of the mental. That philosophical emphasis has spawned many quite different systems, some claiming that there is only the mind and the objects of the mind, others suggesting that at least what we can claim to know is subject to that limitation. And of course, idealism has an opposing view, that of "realism," which in various simple and sophisticated forms emphasizes the reality of the external world as we find it. So, I could imagine someone thinking that "transcendental idealism" refers to a really strong push in that "idealist" direction, "transcending" ordinary "idealism" . . . achieving a kind of "super idealism" where everything is mind in some extreme sense. But "transcend" and "transcendental" are quite different words, and the second one—that you used—is a philosophical term distinct from the ordinary word "transcend." It refers specifically to the new kind of point Kant wanted to make about our relation to "the world."

Y Yes, exactly. The two words, "transcendence" and "transcendental" are related for Kant but have very different meanings. "Transcendence" refers to the outward movement from the self towards the world. "Transcendental" can be understood as a kind of reflective move that attempts to clarify how transcendence is possible at all.

S So, you're not particularly pushing transcendental idealism in this book, but for both Husserl's and your epoché, the issue is to stay with the experience of it and explore that experience—not to give up believing in the external world. And you've said as much already. But if someone isn't careful, it will still be easy to then slide back into thinking that bracketing or suspending belief is the same as disbelieving. And a more subtle potential misunderstanding would be to interpret your epoché in a way that entirely ignores Kant's innovations.

Y It's a common misunderstanding to interpret the epoché as a way of disregarding the external world. But as I just mentioned, "transcendental" means clarifying how transcendence, or going outside of ourselves towards the world, is possible. Both Kant and Husserl were interested in understanding *how* it's possible that we can relate to the world in various ways. They weren't questioning *whether* it was possible.

S Most people, especially nowadays and quite reasonably, tend to think that when someone says something, everyone should be able to understand it . . . or at least *the words*. That's a very democratic attitude. But philosophers have a strange notion of conversations. They mostly have chats with people who are long dead, but who took philosophical positions along certain specific lines, in response to other people at yet other times who also talked and thought about that topic in specific ways. It's a very ancient tradition in Philosophy, still going today. So, Kant, for instance, took up a position in response to those of other philosophers—such as Descartes (as a mind–body dualist and as a rationalist, again in a philosophical sense emphasizing knowledge gained from reason), David Hume (empiricist—"knowledge depends on experience"), Bishop Berkeley (idealist, "knowledge is only knowledge of mind"), and Leibniz (and his followers, emphasizing metaphysics). Kant at a certain point was concerned with finding a balance between those various positions, and avoiding the potential for skepticism (denial of the possibility of knowledge or at least certainty) that he saw in them or as likely responses to them from some quarters. Kant wanted to clarify how our physical senses, our capacity for understanding or judgement, and faculty of reason could all contribute to knowing reality, and to what extent and with what limitations. And how they contribute to real knowledge—not conventional belief—even regarding ethics.

Kant claimed, as central to his more balanced position, that sensory experience and empirically derived data are important for acquiring knowledge, but that more was also required—hence the emphasis on a careful analysis of how judgement and reason also contribute. And more famously, that the presentation of the world of objects around us *conforms* to our cognizing via those latter faculties. He meant this in a revolutionarily fundamental way. The world, reality, is literally a *perceived world*, because categories and structures of our cognition organize and add to what we know. He was not a rationalist in the Cartesian sense, not an empiricist in Hume's sense, nor a naïve realist nor a radical idealist. He was the first transcendental idealist.

As such, Kant ushered in new ways of thinking about the human situation more akin to some perspectives in modern sciences which recognize our human limitations in coloring the world, as you put it, Yuko. Modern science uses an empirical approach plus a lot of technology and mathematics, to extend knowledge and useful theories beyond what Kant could have imagined. And even then, science perhaps still remains subject to some of the cognitive categories he described. In his Copernican Revolution, we don't just get new ideas about the structure and ordering of reality from our cumulative experience of the world, but instead—as a turnabout—we find that the basis or condition of possibility for the experienced world's objects even existing in the way they appear, is our own human cognitive framework. Whether this approaches an "idealist" ontology or just a more sober assessment of our situation is up for debate and future research.

The reason I wanted to elaborate slightly on these background points regarding Kant is that they bear directly on some aspects of Husserl's philosophy that particularly interest me, and on your own approach to the epoché, as well as to Asian contemplative traditions including Zen. But before I comment on any of that, would you like to correct or add to what I've said so far, Yuko?

Y This is a great summary of the context! As you say, philosophers clarify their positions in response to that of other philosophers who lived in the past. So, in order to understand a philosopher's ideas, often it's just not possible if you try to understand it in isolation. You have to look at the problems that they were trying to respond to, which typically takes you way back into history.

Philosophy and Contemplative Practice

S I want to explain a basic point about the epoché and contemplative practice. As just stated, it's important to keep Kant's transcendental idealist view in mind when understanding Husserl. Husserl uses aspects of Kant's basic picture and language, but interpreted it differently in some cases. For us, the main difference regarding Husserl though, is not a matter of his own theoretical subtleties but of his *method*. Husserl saw Kant as offering a perspective that held considerable value, but Husserl also felt that to get at that value, what he called "the copper and gold of it," one had to break Kant. Remarkably, Husserl did that not by offering counter-arguments and analyses in the usual philosophical vein, but by switching to a radically different method—the epoché!

In more casual chats with you at times, you've mentioned that you felt Husserl, through the epoché, had found what you called "a better way of doing philosophy." And I certainly agree that it's an important start. His "turn" in entering Kant's scheme, was towards experience itself, and in understanding that notion somewhat differently than Kant did. You have now taken things a bit further by offering the epoché without the technical trappings that still figure in Husserl's own work. And you emphasized that a main issue is to stay with experience, to keep going on the journey opened up by the epoché. Not to just use it temporarily, as a tool offering a technical insight so that one can then go back to a more standard philosophical analysis or argument.

Y Yes. Husserl opened up a way to explore experience for its own sake. But the exploration there was limited since he had in mind a specific philosophical project. We're freeing the epoché from those limitations which means that, for us, the exploration is also unlimited.

S This is such a big difference that many people often consider it to be incoherent or impossible. At least for the traditions I teach and mentioned in Chapter 5, their main point is that we should learn how much insight and power are actually available in what is ordinarily vaguely referred to as "experience." But in contemplative training, "experience" doesn't just mean what Hume liked to invoke (fact and observation), nor what people call "subjective experience," or subjective idealism. It includes all of life, as it's actually lived.

In my classes and other projects over the years, I've called this an emphasis on an "authentic way of being." We talked about this issue in the last chapter . . . you and I are both emphasizing working with experience and with the particular way one lives and the ways one can live, taking a step further than Husserl's. Buddhism, Daoism, and Confucianism all have generated theories of various sorts, but their primary shared wellspring is the experience side and profound discoveries of authentic ways of being.

With some pointers from the traditions, we can become more aware of what's present in at least ordinary experience and our inauthentic ways of being, the perceptible, felt limitations in the latter. We notice ways of improving our way of being, and of refining our awareness of the inauthentic/authentic distinction. This process, particularly the way it keeps recasting itself on new levels, is a central feature of introductory and intermediate training in all Asian contemplative practice, which is simply lived life, or life lived better.

The process is not vague, ungrounded, disconnected, abstract, or quietist. It's based on initial concrete findings, recognitions of inauthentic actions and mind patterns. Then step by step, everything involved refines and undergoes repeated transformations as more authentic alternatives are sensed. Every aspect of the approach undergoes change, including all of its own schemes or frameworks for interpreting both our practice and our faculties for doing the practice. Contemplative traditions are based on a wide or even open list of emerging capacities for appreciative discernment—knowing.

This is a very different view than Kant's or those of other prominent seventeenth- and eighteenth-century European philosophers. It's not just based on *reasoning*, except perhaps in the beginning stage, but on noticing, seeing, and then on increasingly more direct ways of discerning, using new cognitions for which few or no terms exist in ordinary language. These novel cognitions are also explicitly embodied, not merely "thought."

The richness of this approach is far greater than the standard picture of the "physical senses to start with, then judgement (learning, accumulated knowledge), then pure reasoning" would accept as possible. Kant's way of relating and prioritizing or weighting these three ways of acquiring knowledge differs from Locke's, or Hume's and others, but these philosophers all worked within a similar background picture of our component faculties—the senses, knowledge, the faculty of reason. I could just say contemplative practice gives us new experiences, but that misses a crucial point.

The ordinary notion of "experiences" fits too neatly into various standard pictures as one of our cognitive options, the more empirical one Hume discussed. Contemplative traditions would say this whole scheme or background picture may seem reasonable and adequate for some conventional purposes, but is wrong when assessing the full scope of what we can—with practice—know or discern.

The Contemplative Approach to Ethics

Take ethics as an example of this. A common overview of ethical theory includes Kant's "duty ethics"—using reason to determine moral obligations, plus more consequences-oriented ethics which focus on the status of actions and their ethical status as determined by an action's consequences. A third, more ancient view is "virtue ethics," being an ethical person and acting from that virtuous character. Plato and Aristotle are often mentioned as holding this position.

Traditions of contemplative spirituality are somewhat in the "virtue ethics" camp, using contemplative practice to help people open up their fundamental ethical nature and live from that. The view here is we are all, fundamentally, ethical beings. But this is not much like contemporary philosophical formulations because of the contemplatives' emphasis on intensive practice and personal transformation, enabling a heightened perception of what constitutes an ethical action, resulting in skillful follow-through. Contemplative training focuses on helping people discover their status as thoroughly ethical beings and that their authentic range is much vaster and more deeply founded than is commonly supposed.

So, the issue is acting and living in accordance with that enhanced awareness. And with these practice and transformation points in mind, I could say that all the familiar theories of ethics would be accepted as having a place in traditions like Buddhism, Daoism, and Confucianism. The catch is that the map of cognitive faculties is different here.

Even "awareness" can be an accurate but rather cold word in this context—what's cultivated by the contemplative traditions is also an ethical feeling, in a sense that is not an ordinary emotion. So, let's say "ethical sensibilities" are the point. Again, to even vaguely understand contemplative traditions requires understanding that the common conceptual scheme—sense perception, emotions, accumulated knowledge as information, plus abstract reasoning—fails to cover contemplative discoveries of our full cognitive range.

I've picked ethics as an example because it's a generally familiar issue, unlike more technical or subtle aspects of contemplative spirituality, and thus lends itself to our brief discussion of contemplative traditions where these really do stress ethical cultivation. Stretching the point, much of what's emphasized in Buddhism, even very advanced levels of realization—awakening to a spiritually relevant reality—could be seen as related to ethics. On the more ordinary level, all the traditions and their enhanced perspectives have improved people's ability to practice ethical restraint, keep commitments, live with compassion.

Theories Can Guide, But are not Fundamental

Comparing philosophical theories to contemplative discoveries, consider the issue of philosophical "idealism." No school within Buddhism is much like subjective idealism, but there are idealist ("mind-only") trends to be found in some Buddhist groups.[2] People nowadays often assume Buddhism centers on that orientation, but as I just indicated, our conventional modern picture or framework is too different for that assumption to be right. And on the other hand, empiricist and realist groups can also be found within Buddhism. Kant's more nuanced ideas also echo some Buddhist points.[3] This diversity within Buddhism is possible because different groups were concerned with different spiritual undertakings, and with different kinds of contemplative realizations. They were also guided by different oral and written teachings. Another factor is that contemplative traditions may use philosophical positions on a need-only or temporary basis, as starting points … but the practitioners usually don't believe that texts and teachings (words) can fully capture reality. Words are merely pointers. To offer a variant of a point you just made, Yuko, reality is always a matter of *engaging* reality, not just encoding it in words or systems and then trading only in terms of the latter.

So, idealist, realist, and other schools' contemplatives may all come to a common realization. And if they don't, that may also be simply because people are different and are inclined to somewhat different understandings. This is a fact of life, long acknowledged and accommodated to various degrees within the traditions. At very high levels of realization, some disagreements still remain but usually within a much larger background of agreement. Contemplative practice isn't chaos, where anything goes. It's rigorously constrained, in various ways, depending on the school. Constrained, it seems, by reality.

Here I'm not claiming that contemplative practice provides an alternative or better route to discoveries made by science. Knowing reality is a multifaceted task that will always be our greatest challenge. Frustrations and uncertainties do and will abound. Contemplation won't answer many of the questions with which philosophers or specialists in many other fields have struggled. But contemplatives have been successful in finding extra dimensionality in life and the world by finding extra scope in awareness. And the same applies to the practice of the epoché and reduction that you're explaining.

Y Thanks, Steven. These are all useful points. To close our discussion so far, I'll just mention how I see Nishida fitting into this idealist/realist debate.

Nishida's Philosophical Perspective

Y Nishida is an interesting figure since he's positioned somewhere between philosophy and contemplative traditions. Steven, you mentioned earlier how philosophers like to converse with figures from the past. Well, Nishida engaged with various philosophical figures, from Aristotle and Plato to his contemporaries including Husserl, and, as a matter of fact, much more than people from the Japanese tradition. And of all those people, Kant is probably referred to most in his writings.

In my PhD dissertation, I looked at Nishida's (and Heidegger's) critical engagement with Kant's (as well as Husserl's) transcendental philosophy.[4] Nishida scholarship has tended to emphasize the *discontinuity* between Nishida's philosophy and Kant's transcendental philosophy. This is understandable given that Nishida's philosophy centers around the idea that reality is fundamentally beyond the subject-object duality. He repeatedly says that the subjective viewpoint must be dropped. This certainly includes the standpoint of the transcendental ego. But Nishida didn't outright reject the transcendental standpoint. Rather, he attempted to go beyond what Kant and Husserl had discovered by *radicalizing* it.

Husserl went a step further than Kant in acknowledging the importance of staying with experience and probing into its deeper dimensions. But according to Husserl, experience is always an experience of something *for "me."* Experience presupposes an "experienc*er*." While this may be a natural assumption to make, it's something that must be set aside, according to Nishida. And once we set that powerful assumption aside… or when that assumption spontaneously falls off…reality presents itself in its fullest form. We come into direct contact with reality, where "reality" here means something very different from what we usually mean by it. To refer back to the example I raised in Chapter 2, "I" am not seeing the dancing leaves, but there is simply "the dancing leaves."

Here's a famous line from Nishida's maiden work, *Zen no kenkyū* (『善の研究』, *An Inquiry into the Good*): "It is not that there is experience because there is an individual, but that there is an individual because there is experience. The individual's experience is simply a small, distinctive sphere of limited experience within true experience."[5] This "true experience," which presents reality most directly and fully, is something that we must awaken to. And that's why in my dissertation and elsewhere, I have called Nishida's position, "awakened realism."[6] It's a transcendental position that has broken free from the sovereignty of the transcendental ego.

Whether or not such a position is philosophically tenable is up for debate, but we should keep in mind that like Husserl, Nishida emphasized the importance of staying with our experience and exploring it further. And, coming from a Zen Buddhist background, Nishida was closer to the contemplatives in that this exploration was something to be lived and involved the transformation of the self in the process. Philosophical reflection was therefore a sort of "practice" for Nishida. Reality was really something to be awakened to. I'll have more to say about Nishida in the next chapter.

Discussion Questions

- In this chapter we discuss the historical and theoretical background contextualizing and motivating Husserl's own innovations. How has our view of mind and knowledge changed since Husserl's time? Are recent changes based on psychology or science . . . or something else?
- We looked at how "experience" carries different meanings for Hume, Kant, Husserl, and the contemplative traditions. How do *you* understand the word, and where do you think that understanding comes from? How does your understanding compare to what we mean by "experience" when we speak of "lived experience" and "exploring experience" in this book?
- Do present-day views suffice to ground an understanding of life's meaningfulness and value? How does this book contribute to such understanding, and is yet more needed?

7

Practicing Phenomenology—the Personal Side in Practice and "Play"

Steven (S) Yuko, can you say a bit more about the personal side of practicing phenomenology? In the last chapter, we briefly reviewed bits of the history and theory, and in Part 1 we both gave the reader exercises to try. But it would be interesting to learn more about what it was like for you to work specifically with the epoché.

The Challenge of Really Practicing

Yuko (Y) I'm willing to describe my own attempts to learn about practicing phenomenology. But I still would want to start with Husserl, to provide context. For him, practicing phenomenology actually meant something specific. It was, as we've discussed, *really* about bracketing our belief that the world exists out there outside of us, and then going back to things just as they present themselves to us in our experience. He was actually conducting the phenomenological epoché and the reduction, the two methods that he introduced as part of phenomenological reflection, and describing phenomena from the phenomenological attitude.

So, it was definitely a *practice*, but one that required you to take an unnatural attitude. Therefore, he made a distinction between the natural attitude, where we naïvely believe in the existence of the world, and the phenomenological attitude, a very unnatural one, which required taking up a specific attitude and a kind of discipline to maintain that attitude in order to describe the phenomena from the phenomenological attitude. What Husserl did was introduce these methods, so that anyone could recognize their natural attitude and change it to this unnatural one, to see phenomena just as they appear to us in our experience. So, practicing phenomenology, for Husserl, meant exactly just that.

However, when we talk about phenomenology today in academia, it has a very different sense. The practice part has disappeared, I think. So, what we do in academia today is study phenomenology as a subject in philosophy. So, we learn about Husserl, Heidegger, Merleau-Ponty and so on, all these different phenomenologists, as historical figures. And we learn about the methods that I just talked about. But we never really learn *how* to actually do them, and then put that knowledge to work. The phenomenological epoché and the reduction, we don't actually *do* any of that. We're not encouraged to take up the phenomenological attitude, even though we learn about it.

S The same thing happened sometimes in Asian contemplative traditions, emphasizing doctrine or dogma, history, and specific textual issues, instead of actually investigating it and seeing its real meaning, beyond the words, for oneself. I guess it's just a human tendency to narrow-focus on words and concepts rather than using them as an entry or pointer into the primary, experiential aspect. But it still surprises me. Also, I'm becoming increasingly aware when listening to you talk about "belief" that the issues you mention are very familiar to me, from the traditional contemplative side . . . but with some crucial differences. Perhaps we can come back to that, just to clarify further your own emphasis. But right now, please say more about your own personal attempts to take up the practice Husserl proposed. And about the main things you want the reader to understand regarding the practice.

Y One important difference between the view offered in this book, and the way modern academia works with it, centers on this issue of practice itself—

S As opposed to engaging in academic study? Just really *practicing*?

Y Yes, exactly. Another difference is the extent of the epoché as I'm offering it.

S The *scope* of applying the practice?

Y Yes.

S So, starting with the first point, how did you learn the actual practice?

Y In my view, phenomenology is *essentially* a practice and has nothing to do with studying what people have said in the past.

S (Laughs.) The Ch'an/Zen school would certainly agree with you, for somewhat related reasons. You're saying that to really do it, you had to go beyond what you were taught? Or even beyond all teaching?

Y Exactly. And in my own case, there was never a time in the classroom where we sat down and the teacher said, "Okay, let's all try to really adopt this phenomenological attitude. To really try this on an object." I'm not claiming that no one anywhere does it. I'm sure that's not true. But I personally haven't heard of anyone doing it, or getting such training.

S I've met a couple of phenomenologists who clearly had done the practice as such along some particular line, but not many. What happened in your case?

Y In my courses, initially, I was just trying to understand what was being said. When you read some of the descriptions provided by various phenomenologists, such as Husserl or Merleau-Ponty, they give very precise descriptions of objects and how they appear in their experience. You have to adopt a special attitude in order to really understand what's going on there. So, I started off doing that. But from there, I guess, understanding for me meant leaving the textbook, going outside and looking around, and trying to actually execute this weird, unnatural attitude of bracketing the existence of the world.

S The existence asserted by the mind, in the Kantian sense. This actually goes all the way back to your suggested exercise with the cup, in Chapter 1.

Y Right. And I tried to do that exercise, outside of the classrooms, just on the street, in my room, anywhere. It's a really strange thing to do, and took me a long time to make sense of how it works. I do remember talking to some of my friends at the time and saying, "you know how weird this attitude is and how difficult it is to actually do it?" I remember feeling there's a huge gap between just understanding the descriptions and thinking that you really understand the point conceptually, and then actually trying to suspend the natural attitude. For Husserl it's just one line: "we bracket our belief in the existence of the world." It sounds very simple and straightforward. But really doing that and living it requires a huge effort. Just trying that by itself took me a long time to understand. The process of trying was similar to sitting and meditating.

S Are you talking about a several-year period?

Y Definitely.

S Did you try but fail to apply it sometimes? Or struggle with it?

Y Still, to this day, I don't think it's something that I can adopt all the time. It's such an unnatural attitude, it's something that you have to consciously do, consciously take up that attitude. So, speaking in terms of an "attitude" makes sense in this context, because it is something that you have to adopt, something the reader would have to pick up. And it does require effort to sustain.

S Okay. That's an important point. And would you say that it's gotten any easier? Or is it still very difficult?

Y Yes, it's still difficult. But I eventually realized it had become at least *relatively* easier for me, compared with the initial reactions of other people and students in my class. I always try to get them to adopt that unnatural attitude, but then I see how difficult it is for them. So, I recognize that I've come a long way.

S I recall making the same sort of re-assessment of my own progress, while teaching students from time to time. And the "dancing leaves" episode you described earlier is an example of this shift? Specifically, an example of the phenomenological reduction step, following the epoché?

Y Yes.

Natural and Unnatural

S I mention the connection to the dancing leaves example in particular, because of the Kant–Husserl terminology regarding the unnatural and natural attitudes. From the point of view of my teachers, whether Confucian, Daoist, or Buddhist, it strikes me as strange and even funny that Husserl would describe the ordinary case as "natural" and the more direct case as "unnatural." In the contemplative traditions, the ordinary case is considered "common" or "typical" but definitely not "natural." And the alternative, more cultivated case recommended by the traditions is explicitly considered truly natural—that's the whole point! Dressing down to the more fundamental or "natural."

The Confucian–Daoist–Buddhist traditions would each relate naturalness to a different thing, specific to their tradition's emphasis—being more mature in a human/humane sense, participating more fully in the human relationship to Nature, and awakening from the perverse grip of samsaric habits to the awakened Nature of Mind that's central in Ch'an/Zen. But they all agree that what's on the right track is *natural* in some sense.

Y Right. And I'll be talking about that in Chapter 8, regarding the specifically Japanese emphasis on Nature, in practice and in life.

S Yes. My comment here seems to be just a terminological point, but I think it relates to an important practice tip for the reader too, that while the suspension and reduction are both difficult for us because of our acquired habits, they are not *intrinsically* unnatural or difficult. Rather, they are simple and natural. I admit that initially this kind of re-training involves adopting a new and somewhat artificial stance, but one the traditions would say is eventually seen to be unnecessary once the real—truly natural—way is recognized.

In our previous discussion, you mentioned the phrase "loosening one's grip" which was also a key phrase for my Daoist teacher and one I mention often in my teaching. I think you put it to very apt use, associating seeing the dancing leaves with that loosening. It's then understood as relaxing our involvement in mind-imposed structures, possibly even including ones such as Kant and Husserl described. Contemplative traditions say people can become ungrounded and lose their way under the influence of these structures, and then what is natural and easy becomes hard or even inconceivable. So, we have to re-train back, with some real effort and practice at first, to what is really quite easy and uncontrived—natural. We learn to stay with what is present, in a sense "prior," to the add-ons imported by the ordinary mind.

Y That relates well to my own experience. The difference between the disciplined efforts I was talking about now and the dancing leaves episode is that the dancing leaves experience wasn't something that I consciously even thought about. It's something that just happened. All of a sudden, one of my colored glasses fell off. Actually, I wasn't even looking at the leaves as leaves. I had been trying to understand reality in a specific way I'd heard about from reading the Zen teacher Dōgen, and trying to understand what he was talking about. I was making a conscious effort to drop the mind and body. But I was still in my head at that point, and it wasn't really working. But then all of a sudden, when I looked up, I allowed my eyes to wander and just let all those things I was holding onto go. They fell off. And so what happened there was naturally this epoché, and then naturally, a reduction where I started to see things differently.

S It's actually very normal, probably inevitable, to learn contemplative practice first by studying and concentrating, trying hard to unravel the meaning of a text or teaching, and then spending lots of time doing meditation practice. But it's also normal and actually quite natural, usually during some gap or rest from one's practice, or while performing some mundane chore, to suddenly see the point of the teaching in some central way. The study, effort, formal practice merely potentiate an uncontrived return to something simply present. There are different levels and aspects of what is simply present, but the main point is not complicated. Just as you say. In a sufficiently direct, untainted form, this phenomenological reduction is what Buddhists would call "Suchness." It's central, but usually missed by our being caught up in representations of "me and them," "this and that," "now and then."

Y I was familiar with terms like "Suchness" or the idea of "being simply present" from years of studying Kyoto School philosophy and Zen Buddhism. I had a conceptual understanding of them. And also some kind of an intuitive understanding. But when I saw those dancing leaves in Princeton, it felt like all the concepts fell off and I could just see it directly. Actually. . .I had a similar experience when I had just started studying Nishida. I was basically reading Nishida day and night in the library trying to understand the difficult texts in order to write my undergrad thesis. As I was walking home, I was still thinking hard about what he had said. I stopped at the lights and looked up at the tree next to me. At that moment, for the first time, I felt the presence of the tree in a way I had never felt before. It was my sixth year at the University of Tsukuba and it was the same path I had walked and biked all those years. But it was not until then that I had actually become aware of the tree. For the first time, I understood what Nishida meant by "pure experience." I was probably just standing there, shocked for quite some time. That experience changed the way I relate to Nishida's writings. They were no longer "just words," but gained life. It's interesting that I had this kind of experience at the beginning of my study on Nishida and also right after I submitted my PhD dissertation.

S It sounds like everything came together, and you were ready for the next step!

A Major Conversion

S Traditional Buddhist training systems have formed around the sense that it's hard to work on intermediate or advanced levels of the mind level, seeing what the ordinary mind sets up and then disinclines us to notice. So, they start people on simpler things (bowing, rituals, basic chores done with more awareness, ethics precepts of conduct, many possibilities). They then observe each student in daily life—usually this would be around the monastery. Once a person finally shows signs of becoming more aware of what his/her mind is doing, teachers then give instructions on practices which bring out more of that awareness. So, this literally means that in some groups they don't even start with the now-stereotypical notions of sitting meditation, because those specifically require working on the mind level.

Practicing the epoché, as it's understood in Buddhism, would be part of an extensive mind training regimen, starting with breath and body-energy tracking, and then working step by step with various levels of awareness of mind functions we usually take for granted. Being able to see and work with these processes, habits of thought and reactivity, assumptions, rather than letting them set us up and control us in endless ways. Later, when students' level of awareness is sufficient, they would be trained to see much more subtly held "views" (which bears more directly on the concerns of Kant and Husserl). Practicing the epoché is not easy, but in one form or another, it's going to be important for learning more about living authentically.

Y It makes a lot of sense to me that in contemplative traditions teachers provide different kinds of practices based on the students' needs. You can't just assume that everyone is on the same level, having the same background, same habits and so on. It's so crucial that students receive the right kind of guidance. I have been teaching my students in the past few years how to practice the epoché in my classes. And I see how important it is that they receive the right sort of guidance. It's not easy to identify your own colored glasses and it also helps that we do it together. The students share their experiences with each other, and this helps them get a better sense of what's actually going on when one tries to bracket various beliefs.

S Tailored guidance is usually necessary, but mutual support can also be a big help sometimes. What's at issue here is a big step for anyone. The point you previously made about phenomenological practice leading to a kind of *conversion* seems very central here. You mentioned that many of Husserl's students disagreed with his eventual commitment to a form of transcendental idealism—rejecting the naïve notion that the world exists completely independently of our mind's basic constructs—because it's difficult to see the interdependence and really accept such a counterintuitive, alternate view. It does involve a major conversion in perspective, which many people would probably resist. Actually, I remember reading—and you also mentioned this—that Husserl himself used this word "conversion" to characterize what was involved here and how momentous it is.

Y Yes, that's correct. In what is often referred to as his "last great work," *The Crisis of European Sciences and Transcendental Phenomenology,* written in the mid-1930s, he speaks of the change of attitude to the phenomenological one as a "personal" and "existential transformation" and says it is comparable to a religious conversion.[1] Husserl doesn't explain any further what he really means by this so some deny the importance of this passage. I personally find it very interesting though.

S Buddhist contemplatives would say it makes a lot of sense to put it that way, because they're well aware it's a radical shift in perspective, and even impacts what you think you are. They see that the "me," the apparent self, is set up by habits and tendencies of the ordinary mind. Regarding this, Yuko you once mentioned to me that Kant was not claiming the mind is making or *constituting* reality (a particular version of ordinary "idealist" philosophy) but that it's *contributing* to it in particular ways, which can be studied (the transcendental idealist point).

Y Well, I would say that for Kant, the mind *constitutes* reality in the sense that it *contributes* an essential part of reality. But "constitute" isn't the same as "create." The mind doesn't have the power to just create whatever reality it wants. It's constrained by what is given to the mind from the external world. Becoming a transcendental idealist doesn't mean that you suddenly believe your mind makes up reality. Steven, you mentioned in the previous chapter that some people may misunderstand transcendental idealism to be a kind of "super idealism" where everything is the mind in an extreme sense. This is certainly not what it is. Becoming a transcendental idealist involves recognizing the centrality of the mind's contribution to reality while at the same time understanding that the world or reality puts a constraint on what the mind can do.

S Right, the contribution is constrained. And even then, the extent of it is daunting, shocking. This is a more general view than the one Husserl emphasized. It's not about having a novel experience of some esoteric sort or a highly technical insight about our experience. Rather, it's a very broad-spectrum awareness of all the ways the mind is contributing to our sense of selfhood and the world around us. This awareness impacts our understanding of our emotions, our attachments, habits, recognitions and identifications, judgments, certainties—everything! And to really look into those, or even just to be willing to see them at all, and to understand the implications regarding their shaping influence, and that there's room to go beyond that influence and have a new view ... this is already a classic kind of *conversion* experience precisely because it encompasses everything familiar that we normally take for granted. All the world around us, and much of the mind's activity coloring that world is involved. This is the "scope" issue you started to mention earlier.

Y For Husserl the epoché specifically involved bracketing our belief that the world exists outside of us. But what we've been doing in this book is presenting a more liberal interpretation of the epoché, not just bracketing the existence of bracketing our belief in the existence of the world, but bracketing *any* belief, really. So yes, it's a very broad scope. And I've interpreted the bracketing as loosening our grip. I think this gets at the essence of what the epoché really does—first acknowledge that you have a belief, some kind of idea. And this doesn't have to be just about the world. It can be about yourself, as you just said, or about anything. So, acknowledge that belief, and then loosen your grip on it.

S And its grip on you, as we both are teaching.

Y Yes. Loosening that grip itself may not do much on its own. But what's important is once you've done that, you have a different kind of relationship to your belief. And you have a new kind of openness, an open attitude. This allows you to explore further, to see what the world or life has to offer.

Different Views of What's Possible

S This gets back to some different thoughts I had listening to your earlier comments about "belief." Taking the simplest one, there's a kind of sequence of steps involved here. The first, for Kant, was to call upon our reasoning faculty to perform a special form of argument to *deduce* the involvement of mind-imposed structures shaping the apparent external world. Kant did not believe these structures could be seen directly. But Husserl did. And I'd expect this difference to be hugely important for phenomenology, for your own approach to the epoché, and to contemplative traditions too. It's the key entry to Husserl, then linking to you and finally to the traditions I teach.

Y Yes, for Kant the categories are not something we can see, he derives them through a "transcendental argument." And this is where Husserl criticizes Kant severely. For Husserl, these categories cannot be derived from an argument, or at least not solely. They are something we can directly see, you find them in your experience. This is Husserl's notion of "categorial intuition" he develops in his early two-volume work, *Logical Investigations* (first edition 1900–1901). So, it was present in his pre-transcendental phase, but continued to be important in his later work as well.

S Probably because of my traditional contemplative background, this point has always seemed to be absolutely essential to me—otherwise the phenomenological enterprise seems ruled out. The epoché itself, for example, wouldn't even be possible—how could you suspend what you can't see? Similarly, traditional contemplative practice also depends on seeing more, and specifically seeing what *limits* seeing too!

Y Yes, it's a very important point. And an important difference between Husserl and Kant.

S So, this brings up the sequence bearing on what's special in your approach and how we should locate it relative to Kant or Husserl and also relative to contemplative traditions. First, both before and after applying the epoché, there's the point about seeing. Kant would reject that possibility, Husserl insists on it, and you also agree with me regarding its use. Then the next step is relaxing or loosening your grip on the use of some beliefs or structures that are seen. And that step is another point of departure—Husserl would *not* agree with it, but you accept it.

Y Yes, for Husserl it doesn't make sense to "go open," loosening the grip. The categories are simply things we can see in our experience, and as a phenomenologist you're supposed to describe them. This view was present even in Husserl's pre-transcendental phase.

S OK, so "loosening" is central to your view, but not meaningful for Husserl. And it's also central to the traditions as an initial stage leading to various further realizations, depending on the specific tradition. Confucian and Daoist schools would be more a middle position here, since there are limits to how far they would take the "loosening." But for a Buddhist school like Zen, some subsequent stage along the Zen way would involve completely opening up beyond all limiting views and structures at all levels. So that's a fourth step that's central to some traditions, but I believe this is where your emphasis differs, since you are not concerned with such a total opening across the board . . . nothing too ambitious.

Y Yes, I'm just talking about loosening and then exploring, playing with reality.

S The situation is slightly complicated because Kant and Husserl were concerned with specific categories and structures . . . they may have disagreed about particular items, but these were all largely in line with philosophy and anticipated modern cognitive psychology and related fields in science concerning the mind's biases or basic ways of structuring reality. It should be noted that contemplative traditions do not have that same concern—for example, Buddhists only document and work on seeing and opening up the structures they consider limiting, as I indicated in Chapter 5. That's a different, more specific focus. A similar point could be made for the various Confucian and Daoist emphases.

To use a general characterization acceptable to all three of the main traditions in China, in Chapter 6 I described views, structures and habits as comprising an "inauthentic way of being," a characterization I use quite a lot in my teaching. This focus may occasionally overlap the list of structures at issue in cognitive psychology, but is in most ways quite different. So even for Zen, which emphasizes a radically broad opening, the "loosening and opening beyond" objective cannot be assumed to require overcoming all the tendencies of the ordinary mind that, say, a philosopher or a psychologist of perception studies . . . it wouldn't be necessary to do that in order to deal with samsara, and may not even be possible in some cases. And *in general* it wouldn't be relevant to the spiritual concerns of Zen Buddhism.

For Zen in particular, it's considered possible, relevant, and even essential to relax or open up sufficiently to find a higher cognition that *is itself* always free from some of the ordinary mind's limitations . . . possibly even all of them! But that's a different endeavor from trying to make the ordinary mind per se be free from all of its fundamental tendencies, cognitive filters, and processing systems. Kant may have been right, perhaps the ordinary mind comes with some such structures. People don't need to wipe out or transcend, or even change, the ordinary mind in order to practice contemplation, starting with the epoché. The idea is simply to do enough to leave a space for something fresh to come in . . . a new way of knowing.

Y That's a very important point I would like to emphasize as well. We don't need to think we're going to change the way the mind works. You might want to get rid of some habits, for example, thinking they are bad. The point of the epoché, however, is to just set them aside regardless of whether they are actually bad or not. The idea is not to reject and do away with them, but to simply loosen enough so that there's a bit more space, as you say.

Start with Easy Cases, then Continue

S For our readers, especially if they're just interested in trying some basic experiments with the epoché, my personal recommendation would be to start with the exercises you gave in Part 1 of this book, and then see if any that I mentioned in Chapter 5 also seem enticing. Basically, this amounts to the readers following their own enthusiasm—see where that thread leads. I can personally promise this basic "see, suspend or relax, see more, perhaps fully release where possible" endeavor is possible and valuable. The traditions have been doing it generation after generation in different cultures, for millennia. They too generally proceed by starting with what's easy. If the practice still seems too hard, go back further, to even simpler cases.

To summarize, readers might reflect on this question: what makes a mind habit, attitude, or view a worthy target for the epoché practice? The examples you've given in this book are important because they pick out basic features of human attentional habits that are potentially limiting. Similarly, the ones I mentioned figuring in more traditional practices are targeted because they potentially compromise appreciative awareness.

Examples the traditions would consider important to see, loosen, and even open completely, would be selfishness, heedless grasping beyond truly natural needs, immature reactivity or compulsions, and negative emotions like anger if they're actually proving to be harmful. (See our Chapter 5.) This doesn't mean these limiting tendencies should be eradicated or that they never again arise. What matters is that they're understood better, seen via the "reduction" you've mentioned... so they no longer limit awareness and freedom.

Husserl himself documented a pervasive kind of object-oriented intentionality in ordinary thought, and aspects of this phenomenon would also count as samsara-related targets for Buddhists. This involves more intermediate or even advanced practice. Another example from Husserl's side concerns time structures, right?

Y Yes, he describes the temporal structure of experience. This means any experience has a threefold temporal structure. So, there is the primal impression, which is consciousness of the "now" phase of our experience or of an experienced object. But additionally, our experience doesn't just consist of "now" phases that are merely juxtaposed to each other, in succession. Every "now" phase is accompanied by what he calls "retention." Basically, this means consciousness is holding on to what has just passed. So, there's a part of consciousness in the present that is not just directed to the present, but also holds to what has just passed in our experience. This is "retention." And the "now" phase is also accompanied by "protention," which is an implicit anticipation of what is about to come.[2]

So, every experience has this threefold structure. This is apparent when we take the example of a melody and how we can actually hear it. If you hear tones that follow one another, when you hear one tone in the sequence, you don't only hear the isolated tone, you also are keeping track of the immediately prior tone. And that's why we can hear a melody as a melody and not just discrete tones. This is another example of an essence in our experience. It applies to other experiences as well—perception generally, imagination, memory—all have this structure. Of course, to make such a claim, we have to look into the experience and see if it's really true.

S The same applies with any contemplative teaching. You have to check, verify. Or train until you have the capacity to check and verify ... or reject. Points related to the time structure or chain of events you describe are standard in Buddhist practice, and the idea is to train until you can see it, then train further and learn how to open it up somewhat. Eventually it's possible to find a freedom beyond the chain, or to see that the chain itself is "empty."

But regarding the more basic practice implications, what is your own emphasis for our readers doing the exercises you created? I mean, you're not really telling them to see the categories that matter to Kant or Husserl, nor necessarily everything that would matter to the contemplative traditions.

Y Correct.

S Are you saying they might see some such things, but should also work with other kinds of beliefs or tightly held views, whatever they find and are interested in. And that people can then relax those views to some extent? Does that sum up what you're recommending?

Y Yes, that all sounds about right.

S I'm asking just to clarify your recommendations here as they stand in relation to Kant and Husserl on the one side, and the contemplative schools including Zen on the other.

Y Right. The key point for Husserl is that we don't just see simple things like the color blue. We can see, for example, state of affairs or relations. We can have a direct intuition of them. Phenomenology wouldn't make sense otherwise. This is a huge departure from Kant. And I would want to say something similar, that we can also see various complex relations. So, the important point here, for me, is that there are different kinds of things we can do with this investigation.

S Hence this book!

Y Exactly. So, once we see these things, we can check to see if we can take a bit of a distance from them. And if we can find a way of relating to reality that doesn't rely on them. At least consider it a possibility. It might be that a given complex relation is indeed just part of reality, where there's no way we can get away from it. But the important point for me is that in each case we should try it out, at least to try to loosen or release it. See what we can do. That possibility is not even available for Husserl.

S So, you emphasize experimenting and loosening where possible, but allow that in some cases it might also, maybe eventually, be possible to release some things completely. You want to leave that issue open, I guess.

Y I think so.

S That's very sensible, and realistic regarding what's possible at a given time, always good advice.

Y When you look at it this way, it seems my position is much closer to the contemplative traditions than to Husserl. It's close to Husserl in that I agree we can see the things at issue. But the important thing for me is releasing or opening our grip, which makes it closer to the contemplative traditions. But in terms of any kind of ultimate goal that someone is attempting to achieve, for me, that's a bit open. There's no clear or specific objective, whereas I think in the contemplative traditions there would be.

S You're right. For any given tradition, there would be particular objectives or emphases, as I mentioned earlier. But in teaching students, at a given stage there would still be a wide range of options offered or selected for each individual person. And the rest would be decided based on how the person's practice and experience go over time. Again, our readers should be encouraged to follow their interests, the threads of their discoveries, their enthusiasm. And their intuitions too, even if these are initially fuzzy or not obviously related to the points we're recommending.

Y Absolutely. The most important point is to try it out and to see for yourself. You may not initially know what kind of interests you have and may even question why you need to be doing this at all. That's fine. But if you're willing to try it out, do it and see what it may bring. It's an open exploration, as I've been saying.

The Epoché is Crucial, but Still Just a Tool

S Do you think these issues bear on the reader's approach to your exercises in the early chapters? And to your emphasis on play? To be specific, take our joint favorite, "loosening one's grip." How important is that really, for your approach? And what does it really involve? Starting with its importance, our main message can't just be to keep loosening the way we form around various cognitive structures or habits. I doubt if that's enough to make a life.

Both Husserl and his student Eugen Fink became slightly familiar with bits of Buddhism at a certain point, and when Fink eventually used the epoché to push further, beyond Husserl's preferred territory, he claimed that all the higher realizations in Buddhism also basically amounted to successive levels of applying the epoché. I feel that is an overstatement, since the contemplative traditions' practice involves much more than just "suspending" things, including different levels and kinds of advanced awareness. And many forms of cultivation combine to make contemplative training well-rounded, life affirming, and meaningful. So, while suspending and loosening are important, they are not the only contributing entries into authentic ways of being.

Y Right, loosening is just a tool. It helps us to relate better to reality, to play with reality, which is the main issue. The loosening is just an entry point to that play, but *playing with reality* is what we're aiming for. And the reason why we need to emphasize this point about our grip is because often, we're *not* playing with reality. So there has to be some technique or procedure enabling us to play with reality, like my baby daughter is doing all the time.

S Ah, a reminder about subtle hazards of adulthood. What then do you see happening in the loosening process?

Y I like this image because it nicely captures what happens when we're holding on to some belief. Phenomenologically speaking, there's literally a kind of *gripping*.

S Or being gripped.

Y Yes, it goes both ways. We hold the belief, but it also grasps us tightly. So, our bodies become rigid. For example, you may notice it when you find yourself defending your position to somebody. Your body becomes more *tense*. You holding tightly to your position. Literally. And so, it's not just a kind of metaphorical language, I think it's viscerally how it appears in our body. We can loosen this grasping and being grasped by relaxing it throughout the body.

S Well, that's fun to hear. It's verbatim something I teach in my classes too, especially regarding Daoist practice, which tends to be more physical and energetic. But related points are made in various stages of Buddhist training as well. The only difference from what you're saying is the traditional forms are more technique-based. But as Daoists would be the first to mention, techniques are just a way of becoming re-introduced to your own body and life, at which point the techniques may fall away. The technical instruction is detailed, precise and concrete—pointing to subtleties in holding patterns throughout the living mind–body. With practice we regain the free-form ability to see, feel, and authentically *be* true to more of what we really are, beyond the artifice of any practice.

Y Yes, it's interesting that we don't see this kind of analysis typically in phenomenology, even though you know, it would be a very good complement. If Husserl would have talked about the epoché in these terms, pointing out how beliefs appear in our body—

S And what leads to what, physically and mentally—

Y Right. And what happens when we finally let go. I think that kind of phenomenological account would have been really helpful.

S Over 2,000 years ago the *Dao Te Ching* was already lamenting that people had lost this connection. But now the situation is probably worse—people don't see the way in which the difficulties that they have, or the narrowness or tightness they have, is fully embodied, but can also be released the same way, working with physical intelligence. Tightening up, at least on the levels we're discussing now, is not very hard to see. It must simply be noticed and addressed, partly through a natural response of relaxing and partly by being put in a broader perspective which supports living in a more healthy way. The latter is something which traditions or cultures sometimes help provide, and perhaps we can talk a little about that in the next chapter concerning Japanese culture in particular.

Y Yes, Japanese culture has a unique way of understanding the relation between humans and nature where a "natural way of being" means something quite specific. I'll say more about that in the next chapter.

Full Circle

S Another angle here is while Kant and Husserl both felt we can't escape some basic mind-imported structures, the view you're offering to the reader can actually throw positive light on even that seemingly pessimistic judgment. Because, if some of these structures truly are found to be intrinsic to our lives, part of life's fabric, then the issue is not to get away from them. Rather, we should appreciate them and savor them, or at least learn more about them in an intimately accepting way. Do you agree?

Y Yes, I do. What does it actually mean to say that some structures are intrinsic to the mind? Looking into our experience and studying how the mind is coloring the world is very important if we are to really understand reality and ourselves as part of that reality. And as you say, this understanding would allow us to have a much more open and intimate relationship towards life.

S This may also be part of what your view of "play" means. Also, it's true to phenomenology itself—you're emphasizing staying in the experience of things, and exploring *within* that. Thus, you're actually making a case for phenomenology's main emphasis, taken to its strict conclusion.

Y Exactly. And such appreciative acceptance comes with a sense of wonder, regarding all the complexities of reality. As you explore, you begin to see that the richness was there all along. For reasons we've discussed, you probably won't see it at first, but gradually it becomes noticeable. The exploration becomes fun, and motivates you to even look further and to explore further. Once you start to see more, you can begin to appreciate life for what it is. So yes, that perspective alone is very, very important. Because then the appreciation, the wonder of it all, these push you towards more explorations, without limits. True play.

Discussion Questions

- In this chapter, we discussed personal aspects of practicing the epoché—the initial difficulties and challenges, and recommend starting with easy versions of suspending judgment, related to exercises earlier in the book. Do you feel you can find your own approach to applying the epoché in daily life, and simplifying it when necessary? How would you simplify it?

- Phenomenology emphasizes the importance of directly seeing various ways the mind structures our experience of reality. In Chapter 4, Exercise 2, we tried to get a sense of this by "playing with perception." What were some of the things you discovered about perceptual experience? Do you think you can try to loosen your grip on some of them?
- We talked about how the body gets tense when holding tightly onto your beliefs. Can you observe this tightness in your body? How exactly does it appear to you? Can you try releasing it just a bit, and what happens when you do?

8

Japanese Perspectives on "Practice," "Nature," and "Play"

Section 1: "Practice" in Japanese Philosophy

Steven (S) In the previous chapters, we've discussed some background issues. Our next focus is their expressions in Japan. Would you like to jump in by talking about a central point for both of us: "practice"?

Yuko (Y) Yes, that would be my choice.

S I'm assuming that Japanese philosophy, although it has many distinct and important strands, generally tends to value the practice aspect.

Y Yes.

The Importance of Engagement

S For me practice refers to something exploratory and engaged with life. Everything I sketched out concerning Asian contemplative traditions in general (Chapter 5) was really about engaging with the world in certain ways. Is it safe to assume Japanese philosophy in particular also emphasizes that practice be engaged, experiential, experimental, exploratory, participatory, those kinds of things?

Y Certainly, I agree with much of that. As an example, consider Nishitani Keiji (西谷啓治, 1900–1990), a student of Nishida. Nishitani is a second-generation Kyoto School philosopher. In an essay titled, "On [Matsuo] Bashō" (『芭蕉について』), he explicitly talks about this practice aspect in Japanese philosophy. He also discusses impermanence, or *mujō* (無常) in Japanese, and how the Japanese cultural tradition has always put an emphasis on the transient or transitory nature of things. When we hear the word

Figure 8 Portrait of Nishitani Keiji (1900–1990). AleksandrGertsen, Public domain, via Wikimedia Commons.

"impermanence," it often has a negative connotation. But Nishitani described how the Japanese always saw beauty in impermanence. A lot of the culture therefore developed around this sense, in haiku and art for example. So, there's definitely this sentiment of transience—that values this kind of transience—in the culture.[1]

But according to Nishitani, that sentiment is not yet practice. It's not yet the real practice of transience. For example, when we see beauty in the transitory nature of things, we still detach ourselves from it. We're in a position where we're looking at it and saying, "Oh, that's really nice" and perhaps finding awe in it. But we're then somehow standing apart from that. And so, we ourselves are in a separate, secure, and stable position. To practice this philosophy of impermanence, though, is different—you become *engaged* in the impermanent, seeing yourself as part of this transitory nature of things.[2]

S Yes, because we are, but must make that fact explicit.

Y Right. He was emphasizing that that requires a lot of what you were saying—engagement. And so, practice in that sense. It also requires discipline and is more of a complete *path*. It's not just a one-time thing where you have insight into something and that's it.

S The path is something to be lived.

Y Exactly. The phrase "Japanese philosophy" can cover many things. In my field there's often debate about "Where do we draw the line?", "When did Japanese philosophy begin?" "Are we going to count all these traditions in the past? Or should we start talking about Japanese philosophy in the post-Meiji era, when the word 'philosophy' was invented in Japanese—*tetsugaku*?" This word was translated from the English word "philosophy" and the European idea or form of philosophy was considered important. Should we start calling something "Japanese philosophy" around the time that word was coined? Or should we be more inclusive?

S I've only read a little regarding this distinction and it seemed rife with controversy, as you said. Perhaps we could just take the position that we're concerned here with the sort of philosophy you defined as involving practice.

Y In that kind of view, there's certainly still a continuity within the Japanese tradition. We see a continuity from very early on. It would even include people like the poet Matsuo Bashō (松尾芭蕉, 1644–1694), for example. Bashō was heavily influenced by Zen Buddhism, and people normally wouldn't call him a philosopher. He's mostly a poet and writer. But for him, poetry and writing were very much part of an engaged practice and view. And the same could be said for some of the twentieth-century Kyoto School philosophers as well. Especially the ones we've mentioned—certainly Nishida, Nishitani, and Ueda (a third-generation Kyoto School philosopher). For all of them, this practice aspect, in the sense of really engaging the self, putting the self into the equation, was important. And being engaged and exploring this path, that too was a central part of their philosophy. So yes, I certainly agree that there is an emphasis on practice in Japanese philosophy.

S In contrast to a more abstract science-like philosophizing about a separate world that one can reason about, versus a world you actually participate in.

Y Right.

S Bashō actually showed how to participate. He didn't rationally describe it, he just showed doing it. Or being it. With Bashō, you're jumping in the pond with the frog, splash!

Figure 9 Portrait of Matsuo Bashō (1644–1694) by Hokusai. Hokusai, Public domain, via Wikimedia Commons.

Y Yes! Regarding our earlier comments about practicing phenomenology, I should add here that originally for Husserl, phenomenology was a practice of sorts. But the word "practice" may mean something slightly different there. And we've also mentioned how for Husserl, phenomenology was a discipline that evolved. Early on it was more of a foundation for science, but later, Husserl wanted to put life in the equation. Finally, we've said his turn to transcendental phenomenology was a big shift—the path opened up. To go transcendental, for me, essentially, is to put the self into the equation. And so, the path, at least in principle, opens up to a larger sense of practice. But when we talk about practice in Japanese philosophy, its proponents have really emphasized a value to practice in the sense of ongoing living. There's a sense that such practice can be *deepened*. And I'm not sure whether phenomenology as practiced by Husserl could really be a deepening, or could have this deepening dimension.

The part that we've extracted in this book, practicing the epoché to open up to reality, I think that's the essence of the phenomenological epoché. And yes, it's exploratory and there are many different ways it can open up to reality. So, there's certainly a deepening component there. But for Husserl, I don't know. He may not have been happy with this idea. He would have wanted a more rigorous and focused definition of the epoché, which would limit its scope. The word "practice" didn't carry the same sense. But certainly, what we mean here by practicing phenomenology has the same sense as in Japanese philosophy.

S So, you feel this is one of the main underlying motives behind some Japanese philosophy and phenomenology?

Y Yes. And following up from there, I think we might look even more closely at the issue of transience.

The Centrality of Impermanence in Japanese Philosophy and Culture

Y I've mentioned Nishitani Keiji and how he talks about this notion of *mujō* (無常) in Japanese. "*Mu*" (無) is the negation, and "*jō*" is the kanji for permanence, so *mujō* means "impermanence." He says this notion itself is not something that's exclusive to the Eastern traditions. It's a rather universal idea that people in general have to deal with. But whereas in the West people have tended to seek some sort of permanent, absolute, unchanging principle, or even God, behind the impermanence that would transcend the impermanent nature of things, in the Eastern traditions this was not the case. In particular, the Japanese have looked at the "bottomless" (*soko ga nai* 底がない) transient nature of things.[3] Not really seeing anything behind it, but interestingly, without that leading to a simple nihilistic worldview. Rather, it has kind of turned around ... when you push this bottomless impermanent nature of things, it reaches a point where it becomes acceptable and even beautiful. Somehow it takes on a positive meaning.[4]

S Yes. That relates to what you were saying earlier.

Y Yes. The other word for impermanence or transience is *hakanai* (はかない). These words, *mujō* and *hakanai*, were not used negatively but rather positively in the tradition. This word *hakanai* is quite interesting. "*Nai*" (ない) is a negation and "*hakaru*" (はかる) means "to measure" and it also means "to plan things out." So etymologically it means that it cannot be measured or it cannot be planned, which suggests that the transient nature of things is beyond what humans can control and manipulate … which leads to the Japanese notion of "nature" or *shizen* (自然) … nature as having its own course of being and how things have a natural way of unfolding. So, there's this kind of acceptance of the natural unfolding of things that are beyond human control. I'll talk more about *shizen* later in this chapter.

S I do recall in the past your mentioning that you would like people to understand the use of the epoché in this book as being ongoing, not having an endpoint. And that seems to relate to what you're saying here too.

Y Right. It's an ongoing practice. The point of the epoché is to play with reality. And playing with reality can have various dimensions and depth. Letting nature play is one way in which we can play with reality. And tuning into nature is one way of practicing the epoché.

S Daoists would certainly agree. For them, it's the primary way.

Y Right, and there are other dimensions of the play of reality. Not just nature but also interpersonal relationships, as we've both mentioned earlier. It goes back to our point that really this is a practice and as such there's no real endpoint at which we can say "Okay, that's it. We've reached the end. We've accomplished it and we can now stop." I can't really conceive how that would be possible.

S People might think they've reached the end, or want to stop, but those are, again, more habits of mind than good assessments.

Y This idea of *mujō* or *hakanai* and the Japanese acceptance of the impermanent nature of things and appreciation for it … I think it all has roots in various traditions, but I think one primary example is the Zen Buddhist tradition.

S Yes.

Y So, I'll be curious to hear about that. You've mentioned to me that the way Zen Buddhists deal with this idea of transience is quite different from the early Buddhist notion.

S I was referring specifically to Dōgen. Yes, I could make a few quick comments about that shortly. But for now, please continue.

Y All right. I was just thinking about things related to this practice aspect, such as the case I mentioned in Chapter 2, about how Japanese describe getting married. Saying "things have happened such that we have become married" sounds strange in other cultural contexts. Very passive. But this relates to what I mentioned earlier about nature. Of course, getting married is something that you decide, but at the same time, there's an understanding and appreciation that without the natural unfolding of things, without a greater force than the human, this would not have been possible. Meeting the special person, at the right time and place . . . this sort of event is not really something that you can intentionally bring about. So "getting married" wouldn't have happened without a greater force in play.

S Right.

Y So, there's this very intimate connection to nature and to the natural way things unfold for the Japanese people. Perhaps people in some other cultures today are not so aware of this aspect, not really appreciating that there is a greater force in play and that things wouldn't have been possible otherwise. And I think many Japanese are oblivious of it too, even though the language embodies this kind of understanding. But if I were to explain it in those terms, in this way—

S —to Japanese people, you mean? They would get it.

Y Yes. They will say "Oh, yes, it's true!" And they would probably give other examples where we talk in this way because it's so engrained in our language. The auxiliary verb "*reru*" (れる) and "*rareru*" (られる) is another good example. This auxiliary indicates several different things including the potential form, being able to do something, and the spontaneous occurrence of something. For example, we say, "*Watashi ni wa sou kanjirareru*" (私にはそう感じられる), which can be translated as, "It feels that way to me" or "I can feel that way." We can also say, "*Watashi wa sou kanjiru*" (私はそう感じる), "I feel that way." But in the former expression, there is a sense that the feeling is something that came spontaneously from somewhere else, not something that I willfully brought about. Here again, we see how the Japanese people traditionally saw an intimate connection between the human way and the natural unfolding of things.

S It's a very good point.

Y This step, this practice, I think, for the Japanese-speaking people is not so far away. This is clear once one becomes a bit more aware of the language, and how much our language reflects the tradition. Actually, the passive way of speaking in Japanese sometimes leads to a denial of personal initiative and responsibility. So, then the feeling is not really "mine," but something that came to me "naturally." But I think this is based on a mistaken understanding of what "nature" and "natural" mean traditionally. To partake in the natural unfolding of things doesn't mean we give up being responsible agents. I hope this will become clearer later when I talk more about the Japanese sense of nature.

Going back to Nishitani, I mentioned he compared a Western penchant to look for permanence behind impermanence, whereas in Japan there's been a tendency to accept the impermanent nature of things just as they are in their impermanence. And together with that goes a warm appreciation and care towards this transience. Adding to that was the example he raises, which is the phrase "*mono no aware*" (もののあわれ). It's a quite well-known phrase, but it's also untranslatable.

"*mono no aware*": *mono* means "things" and "*aware*" is an expression of being moved or touched.

Sometimes it's understood as the awe of things or the pathos of things. And this sense was predominant in the Heian period, from around the end of the eighth century to the early twelfth century. You can see this idea in songs, haiku poetry, art, and literature. Motoori Norinaga (本居宣長, an eighteenth-century eminent scholar on Japanese classics) wrote extensively on "*mono no aware*" and studied how central it is in Japanese culture. "*Mono no aware*" according to him expresses the way "*kokoro*" (心) or heart–mind is moved in delight or in sorrow when touched by things. Nishitani says, regarding this awe of things, that the basis of it is, again, the transitory nature of things.[5]

A typical example of "*mono no aware*" is cherry blossoms, or *sakura*. They start to blossom around the end of March or beginning of April, but only last about a week. Even today, there are countless songs about *sakura*. This love for cherry blossoms is characterized by a sadness, sorrow, because they are so transient. But at the same time, there's a warm, tender feeling that goes with it. That's characteristic of any feeling we have towards this impermanent nature of things, and "*mono no aware*" really captures that sentiment of transience.

Returning to my comments on Nishitani, he mentioned that having that kind of sentiment is not yet practice of *mujō*, transience. He claims that when we are moved by the transient nature of things, we're still looking at it from the outside, standing in a secure position, outside of the transient nature of things, thinking that "I'm not really part of that transience."

To practice *mujō* or transience, on the other hand, is to not only accept this transitory nature of things as transitory, but to throw yourself into the transience. To put the self into the equation.

Here Nishitani is still generally talking about how Buddhism deals with transience, and what it means to practice transience from a Buddhist standpoint. But he's also talking about all of this as it relates to people in the Japanese culture. So, I'm guessing that Buddhism here mostly means Buddhism as it was received in Japan.

S Or developed over time, sure. I'm much more familiar with Buddhism as it unfolded elsewhere, and I agree the Japanese perspective you've described is special.

Y He also wrote an essay about practice, titled "On Practice" (「行ということ」). And reading that, I realized that it's very important to note this word "practice," a word in Japanese that I'm using, and a word that's used by Nishitani, which is *gyō* (行). *Gyō* (行) is actually a Buddhist word. I think the Sanskrit equivalent is "carita." I believe it means practice, or "sadhana."

S Yes.

Y So, it's the word for spiritual exercise or training. Besides that word *gyō* (行), we do have a different word in Japanese that also means "practice" or "application," which is *jissen* (実践). But that's a more modern word that was introduced to contrast with "theory." This word *gyō* (行) that Nishitani is using is specifically coming from a Buddhist context, and I think Nishitani is definitely using it in that sense. In the beginning of this essay, he says that one of the unique features of modernity is that the practice element has dropped out of human development.[6]

Types of Knowledge

S In our earlier chapters, we've both talked about how—as you put it—the practice element has dropped out. This has happened in European philosophy and then phenomenology.

Y Right. Regarding that, Nishitani adds that scientific knowledge has become the predominant form of knowledge. "Scientific knowledge" here refers to knowledge of objects, where even subjects are taken to be objects. And there's no longer the kind of knowledge where knowledge of things and knowledge of the self are inseparable. By the latter, he's describing a way of getting to know things where the self is transformed from within. This transformed self, in turn, allows for a deeper understanding of things, which further transform the self, and so on.

This kind of knowledge is very different from scientific knowledge, where again, the self doesn't come into the equation. He discusses two features that are unique to this knowledge, which is practice-based. The first one is that an important part of this knowledge is knowing the self, or self-awareness. The second important feature is that it is always embodied—the body is always an important part of this kind of knowledge.[7]

So Nishitani is saying this kind of knowledge, where the knowledge of things and knowledge of the self, are inseparable has disappeared, obscured by the scientific knowledge which has become predominant. And therefore, when people now speak of knowledge, they're thinking of theoretical knowledge, and not really thinking about practice. No longer thinking about how this knowledge can transform the self or how the body can come into play in this knowledge. And he also shows how *gyō*, practice, that originally belonged to the religious realm, then spread into the lives of secular people, where they could speak of the *shugyō* (修行) of the various *dō* (道) practices. *Shugyō*, which is another word that means spiritual practice or training, is actually a very common word that we use in our daily life. We would say to an apprentice, "*Shugyō ga tarinai*!" (「修行が足りない！」) meaning, "You need more training!" All kinds of *dō* practices, like *Budō* (武道, martial arts), *Geidō* (芸道, art practices), *Sadō* (茶道, tea ceremony), *Shodō* (書道, calligraphy), and *Kadō* (華道, flower arrangement), have the word "path" in them. They are all paths to be lived and practiced. It's very similar to religious or spiritual practices in the sense that, of course, the body is involved, but also there's a self-transformation involved. That's very much a core part of that practice. And he says the fact that it has spread into the general culture, beyond the religious context, is unique to Japan. Steven, do you want to comment on any of this?

S You've touched on a lot. I'll just mention quickly that the most common Indian Buddhist views of impermanence do reflect what you've said. But they also differ a bit. They center on warnings regarding attachment to things and even the self, thinking of them as permanent when they aren't. The point there is to cultivate awareness of mistaken notions of the human situation, which lead to attachment. So, as you indicated, this involves practice that helps see clearly what life is and what the self is too, and undergoing self-transformation as a result. In theory, this Buddhist point doesn't amount to saying impermanence is a bad thing, just that it can be a problem when people don't realize that they're still clinging to views and desires based on the assumption things are permanent. But even in some Buddhist texts one finds impermanence cast in a negative light, whereas Nirvana, by contrast, is said to not change or fall apart. "It won't let you down." So, in some groups, a form of "detachment" is emphasized as the alternative to "attachment." We're recommending participation as a better approach.

On a higher level of standard Buddhist Mahayana and other teachings, engagement, acceptance, and full participation in life are more primary points, but I think the Japanese perspective includes unusual appreciative and aesthetic emphases even there. And in Zen—Dōgen Zenji for instance—we see a delight in turning Buddhist traditional ideas on their head. So Dōgen describes impermanence as a positive thing, a source of inspiration, that actually aids enlightenment rather than constituting a flaw to which we must become reconciled. This involves an advanced contemplative insight, but is an example of staying with the full dimensionality of reality we're in rather than getting caught in partial unchecked views or frozen dogma. That's only possible with full, awake participation. So, I guess it's in line with what you're saying about practicing phenomenology—staying with the experience!—and with your points about Japanese thought more generally.

Integrating Philosophy, Scholarship and Contemplative Practice

S Coming back to your presentation, could you say more about the issue of practice and how it relates to philosophical reflection?

Y This is something that comes up with Nishida and Nishitani. And it relates to some comments by Ueda Shizuteru too—he's a third-generation Kyoto School philosopher who passed away only a few years ago. Ueda speaks of Nishida as a Zen practitioner philosophizing, and a philosopher practicing

Zen. I find that statement quite revealing. On the one hand, he's saying Nishida was a Zen practitioner. Nishida meditated very seriously for about 10 years, really committed to Zen, practicing at home, but also going to temples and meditating. And even after that, he continued. It was a lifelong practice for him. So, Zen specifically was always a base for him. And that's also the starting point for him as a philosopher. So that's him, as a *Zen practitioner* philosophizing. But at the same time, he's a *philosopher* who is practicing Zen. Nishida was not content with just practicing Zen. As you know, Zen emphasizes not reflecting too much or not thinking too much. This practice of non-thinking was one of the important aspects of Zen. And Nishida was never really happy with that aspect of Zen.[8]

S In Chapter 3, you mentioned this as a "letting go of thinking" and as suspending it, practicing the epoché. Those are good characterizations, and can be part of a balanced approach. Often though, this notion that Zen, or higher-level Buddhist contemplative teachings in general, opposed any reliance on thinking is very common. It has been taken too far. The real point behind it is simply that for advanced contemplation, especially during formal sitting practice, the ordinary mind (including thinking as a mental activity training in words, concepts, memories, preferences, habits, and attitudes) is seen as such but not used. Not followed. Instead, one relies on a more truly fundamental, higher kind of awareness and insight, which I've mentioned previously. This reliance doesn't really rule out using thinking in philosophy or other intellectual disciplines. It simply means one shouldn't expect too much from the ordinary mind. My own teachers just said "for some things, you need to use memory, thinking, logic, and calculating, so go ahead. Once you're done, come back to real (higher) awareness." Each has a place.

Y For Nishida, it was important that he articulated some of the insights of Zen Buddhist philosophy, in a philosophical manner and in dialogue with European philosophy. So, in that respect, he is a kind of European philosopher. But again, he's not just any European philosopher. He really wanted to bring this reflection back to the origin, which means reflecting on the fundamental aspect of reality, which is for him "pure experience" or beyond the subject-object duality, beyond reflection. This starting point, the fundamental basis of reality, is not something that you can reach through philosophical reflection. And in that regard, you have to go beyond the normal scheme of philosophy.

S So, he was using both Zen contemplation and the commitment to philosophy and follow-through within that philosophical undertaking, as a kind of an integrated approach of some sort.

Y That's right.

S How unusual is that integrated approach, in Japanese philosophical history?

Y Well, according to Ueda, this encounter between Zen and philosophy, which was really initiated by Nishida, is something that was unprecedented. So, Nishida would be the starting point of Japanese philosophy in that regard.

S In India and in Tibet, this integration of the commitment to a kind of philosophical investigation and clarity, and analysis, for example, would be seen to be naturally a part of the larger picture of studying Buddhism and practice, all the way to very advanced realization. So, within that framework, you'd have some people who were specialists in the practice, I mean, they weren't suited to be philosophers. Other people were very interested in philosophy and not very good at practice, or even inclined to do much practice. But the tradition tended to be most impressive when embodied in at least some people who were able to do both. That was the mainstay of parts of Indian and Tibetan Buddhism. What you're saying Nishida did would be considered very normal when viewed in that context, for Indian Buddhism from say, around the beginning of the Common Era, through something like the twelfth century. And then after that, it fell off drastically, while being picked up again, and becoming strong in Tibet during some centuries. Later it flourished, intermittently, in Mongolia. That's pretty normal for these traditions, they sort of "spark" . . . they come alive and are incredibly creative for a while, and then they fade back to just little glowing embers, sometimes almost nothing. And then they spark up again, later, somewhere else. I guess that's just the way human development runs, in general.

Y So, what Nishida was doing isn't so extraordinary in the context of Buddhist history. That's interesting. It's also interesting that historically, the practice bit and the philosophy bit often come apart. Nishida took up an integrated approach and so did a lot of his followers, but most of us who study Nishida today are "Nishida scholars" who have little interest in actually practicing Zen.

S Perhaps Japan emphasized certain points that you don't see as much elsewhere. Or certain points were integrated into the larger Japanese culture in a way that you don't see elsewhere. For instance, in India and Tibet, some people were incredible specialists in the philosophy side, they would study in great detail certain philosophical subjects for 20 or 30 years as part of an academic program some monasteries were running. And then after all of that training, some of them would start doing meditation practice. That's hard to imagine in the busy modern world. But my point is that the more general culture of some "Buddhist countries" wasn't concerned with this kind of specialized development. Whereas in Japan some things the philosophical specialists were doing may have reflected points that had already been kind of picked up in the culture, or they may be kind of drawing out things that had started to become part of the culture. Or they may have contributed borrowings from the culture back to the culture in heightened forms. That's for you to say, but you see what I mean. There are some cultures that were heavily influenced by these contemplative traditions in certain ways, while others weren't. I'm guessing Japan is an example of a society where there were a lot of interactions in both directions.

Y Definitely. I have heard that Nishida's maiden work, *Zen no kenkyū* (善の研究, *An Inquiry into the Good*), first published in 1911, is still the most widely read philosophy book in Japan today. I don't know if that's really true, but in any case, I do think that Nishida's idea that "pure experience," or the direct experience prior to the subject-object duality, is the true nature of reality resonates with a lot of people. And this probably has something to do with the fact that contemplative traditions have seeped into the Japanese culture.

What's interesting from my point of view is that I am a specialist in Kyoto School philosophy, but not really in the Japanese tradition, or in Japanese religion. So, I often hesitate to really talk about anything beyond the Kyoto School philosophy, pre-Meiji period. But inevitably, when I start expanding on the background to Kyoto School philosophers, I have to draw on this other material. There's definitely a continuity that cannot be ignored. You know, a lot of people like to draw a clear line between pre-Meiji period and post-Nishida, saying that "this is clearly something different" and "this is where philosophy begins." But that's quite arbitrary. The deeper continuity is going to be important to really understand what these philosophers were getting at.

S The possibility of what I called an "integrated approach" linking philosophical thought and contemplative practice or insight derives from the fact that contemplation is actually, and properly, many things. To embody both philosophical acumen and contemplative insight is possible because the boundary between them is quite fuzzy. I can say that, even though in another sense higher contemplative awareness is something very specific and unique, an aspect of reality according to the traditions, and is clearly distinct from ordinary "thinking." But thinking can itself be focused, precise, and probing deeper and deeper, stripping away distracting add-ons and then sensing, intuiting, revealing very important things. And this in turn can be a door into higher contemplative awareness. Many philosophers in history have reported passing through this door. Both philosophers and scholars in the traditions have always played a very important role, framing and guiding contemplative practice.

Yuko, although we've talked about how people in academia have sometimes dropped actual practice and just focused on conceptual frameworks, would you agree that philosophy and scholarship are still vital to the larger enterprise of leading collective understanding, even experiential understanding, forward?

Y Definitely. We've talked about how the historical background is important for understanding philosophical concepts. Some scholars study the formation of certain ideas and the influences of certain philosophers and texts. These studies are quite often very specific and detailed. It may seem like they are only interesting for academics, but they play an important role in expanding our general understanding of the ideas.

Contemplation is Important for Everyone

S The English word "contemplation" is a good example of what we're discussing. It can mean "to think about" something. It's that simple. And even in the contemplative traditions it can be just that—you start there, maybe considering a line from a text, and stick with it. Drill into it. This itself is a classic contemplative practice. Good scholarship is too. A scholar might think "Well, what kind of point is this one? And is it related to that other point I was reading, or maybe to some others elsewhere? And what's the best way to understand what's involved in all of these?"

So, my main point here is that even if our readers do nothing but read bits from this book, and then consider a few points and passages carefully, incisively, especially in a life-related context, that's great! From the traditional point of view, that's already contemplation—"practice"—and can open further to higher kinds of contemplative awareness too.

Y I couldn't agree more! If you come across a passage that somehow speaks to you, I would advise to just stop there, put the book down, and just think about it for some time. Go for a walk or a coffee, think more about it and how it relates to your life. This is basically what I do when I read philosophy books.

I go over the same passage over and over again or I come back to it after thinking about it for a few weeks, months, and sometimes years.

S The main thing is just to do your best along whatever line is natural for you. There are a lot of possible forms of contemplation, and many are just part of ordinary life.

The Contemplative Dimension of Travel

Y Working with impermanence can be one way to bring contemplation into various aspects of ordinary life. For instance, you can practice understanding impermanence by traveling. Bashō showed this very well. He wrote about it in a travel diary titled *Oku no Hosomichi* (奥の細道, originally おくのほそ道), "The Narrow Road to the Deep North," published after his death. It's in both prose and haiku. He went on a long journey, for about 150 days, totaling about 2,400 kilometers on foot. A long trek in those days, and very difficult as well. The first lines of this are very famous: "*Tsukihi wa hakutai no kakaku ni shite, yukikau toshi mo mata tabibito nari. Fune no ue ni shōgai o ukabe, uma no kuchi toraete oi o mukaurumono wa, hibi tabi ni shite tabi o sumika to su. Kojin mo ōku tabi ni shiseru ari* (月日は百代の過客にして、行かふ年も又旅人也。舟の上に生涯をうかべ、馬の口とらえて老をむかふるものは、日々旅にして旅を栖とす。古人も多く旅に死せるあり。)." Probably all Japanese can recite the first part by heart. The translation goes: "The days and months are travelers of eternity, just like the years that come and go. For those who pass their lives afloat on boats, or face old age leading horses tight by the bridle, their journeying is life, their journeying is home. And many are the men of old who met their end upon the road."[9]

So, traveling for him was a way of engaging with the transient reality. You have new encounters when you travel, but it's quickly followed by a goodbye. So, his travel is a kind of practice of not becoming attached to things. Letting go, no permanent place.

S Great point. So, would this be an example of something that you'd recommend to our readers as a clue about how they can see their own lives?

Y I would raise a question: when we travel nowadays, do we ever really practice impermanence? Understanding there's no permanent place? And the answer is probably "no."

S Not if we can avoid it!

Y (Laughs.) Right. When we go somewhere new, sightseeing, we immediately get our phones out and try to keep that moment alive, permanently on our phone and on the internet and so on.

S True.

Y This is a point that Nishitani makes somewhere as well. When you go to a new place, most people are not really seeing things. They may just be looking at the surface. They're enjoying the fact that they're in a new place, but they're not getting in direct contact with the reality that's being offered to them. And that could be for various reasons, but perhaps they're just happy to be away from their everyday lives, in some new place. So, they're happy being away from their daily concerns. But in doing so they're actually not really leaving behind their concerns—those are still in the background. For Bashō, traveling meant something very different. But how many of us could really do this today? It would require a very different relationship with life when traveling, and more understanding of what traveling shows.

S So, the readers might also do well to consider how this relates to them in life when they're *not* traveling, just at home dealing with ordinary things, the basics of day-to-day life.

Y Definitely. And here I'll mention a small, related point—the Japanese word for "goodbye." A lot of people at least know the word "sayonara." The etymology is quite interesting. It comes from the word, "*Sayou naraba* (左様ならば)." It means something like, "if that is the case." It's a very interesting phrase to use at the end of an interaction when you say goodbye to people. "If that is the case. . ." The idea here is that you are acknowledging what has happened in that encounter with the person, and then you're open to whatever may follow. It's not a complete closure.[10] This is a very interesting way of saying goodbye, and I think it relates to understanding impermanence. Something is going to happen next; things are going to change. And what you're doing is acknowledging this "being in transition" aspect when you say sayonara!

Section 2: The Japanese View of Nature

In the previous chapters, and earlier in this chapter, I mentioned that the Japanese have a specific sense of nature. Here, I would like to expand on that. I'll start with an analysis of the Japanese word for nature, which is *shizen*

(自然). "Nature" in English is typically understood in contrast to things that are artificial or to the human world. This is very different from what the Japanese understand with the word *shizen*. In the Meiji period, this word was adopted as a translation of the word "nature" in English, but the word existed before that. It is written in the same way, but it was read differently—*jinen*. The word *jinen* stands for the Daoist sense of nature. We can see traces of this Daoist sense of nature in the *kanji* (the Chinese characters) that are used. "*Shizen*" or "*jinen*" is comprised of two Chinese characters, "*ji*" or "*shi*" (自) and "*zen*" (然). The first character is a prefix meaning self and the character is used in words like "*jiko*" (自己) or "*jibun*" (自分) which both means "self" or "myself." The character can also be read as "*onozukara*" (おのずから). "*Onozukara*" is an adverb that signifies that something occurs naturally of itself. So, we would say, for example, "*onozukara akiraka ni naru*"(おのずから明らかになる), which means that something has become clear by itself, on its own. The second character "*zen*" (然) is also read as "*shikari*" and it means "to be so." It's an affirmation of something. So just looking at characters, the meaning of *shizen* is "to be so of itself." It's an affirmation of what something is of its own accord.

At this point, I think there are two points that are worth noting. The first is that this first character "*ji*" or "*shi*," which I said can be read as "*onozukara*," can also be read as "*mizukara*" (みずから). And *mizukara* means that something is done by oneself. So, an example in ordinary speech is "*mizukara erabu*" (みずから選ぶ) which means I choose something by myself and not someone choosing for me, for example. What's interesting is that in traditional Japanese thought, the word *mizukara* and *onozukara* are closely related words. The fact that the same Chinese character is used to signify these two different meanings shows how close they are. Bret Davis, who's a scholar in Japanese philosophy and Zen Buddhism, has an article on nature and freedom in Japanese thought and he talks about what he calls "the nonduality between the personal initiative that's implied in *mizukara* and the impersonal naturalness implied in *onozukara*."[11] The point here is that although these things can be distinguished and, in fact, they usually are separate, in traditional Japanese thought, there is a sense that they are deeply connected and cannot really be thought apart.

The second point is that the word *shizen* was originally used as an adjective ("*shizen na*" 自然な, natural) or adverb ("*shizen ni*" 自然に, naturally) and not as a substantive. This means that people understood nature, not primarily as things in nature or as denoting a region of natural things, but rather, as *the way things are*. And, importantly, this includes the way humans are. In fact, Japanese tradition has emphasized that this kind of "naturalness" is the authentic way in which things are and one that humans should strive to regain. This is because most of the time, we are not natural; somehow, we are "unnatural." So, what we need to do is to try to achieve the "naturalness" that is originally in us but has been lost.

I think that even today Japanese people have a sense of the two points I just mentioned. When we speak of *shizen*, it is of course often used as the equivalent to the English word for nature, where it is understood to be opposed to the human world. But generally, people also have a sense of the other meaning that can be traced back to the Daoist tradition. They may not be aware that this word comes from the Daoist tradition. Nonetheless, they still have a sense of this naturalness as a way of being. When I explain this to my Japanese students, for example, it isn't so difficult for them to understand since this "sense" is somehow still part of the culture.

Section 3: Interpreting the Ten Oxherding Pictures

Ueda Shizuteru (上田閑照, 1926–2019), a third-generation Kyoto School philosopher, gives an analysis of the idea of "*onozukara*" in his commentary on the Ten Oxherding pictures. I would like to introduce his analysis here as I feel it's helpful to get a better understanding of the Japanese sense of nature.

The Ten Oxherding pictures are something that is used in the Zen Buddhist tradition to help understand the path to realizing the true self. There are other similar oxherding picture sets that consist of five or six pictures. But I believe that the most widely circulated one in Japan, at least to my knowledge, is the Ten Oxherding pictures, and specifically the one created by the twelfth-century Chinese Zen master, Kakuan Shion (廓庵師遠). It starts off with a picture of a man who's looking lost. He then spots the footsteps of an ox—which stands for the true self—and attempts to catch it. Upon successfully catching it, there is the stage of taming, then becoming one with it, and then eventually, in the eighth picture, everything is gone. Both the ox and the man disappear from the picture. There is only an empty circle. What immediately follows is a picture of nature. A tree blossoming alongside a river. And the tenth picture shows two people, an old man and a young man, that seem to be exchanging something. Steven would be in a better position to explain in more detail the historical background of these pictures. What I want to do is to talk about how Ueda refers to these Ten Oxherding pictures in discussing this sense of nature that we find not only in the Zen Buddhist tradition, but also in Japanese thought.[12]

Ueda focuses on the last three pictures and says that they form a triad. These pictures are not to be understood separately. And Ueda says that these

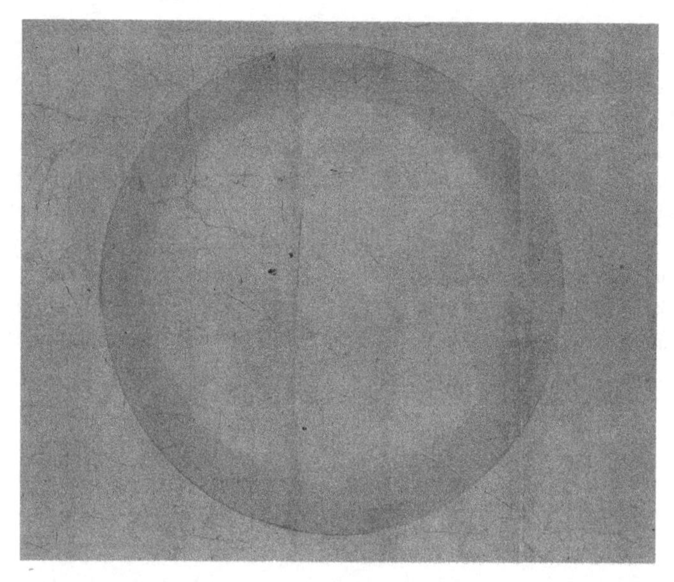

Figure 10 Drawn by Tenshō Shūbun (天章周文, 1414–1463) in the Muromachi period. Titled, "*ningyūgubō*" (人牛俱忘, The Ox and the Man Both Gone out of Sight). The English translation of the title is D. T. Suzuki's from *Manual of Zen Buddhism*. Postcard, Courtesy of Jotenkaku Museum, Shōkokuji temple. Public domain, via Wikimedia Commons.

Figure 11 Titled, "*henpongengen*" (返本還源, Returning to the Origin, Back to the Source). Postcard, Courtesy of Jotenkaku Museum, Shōkokuji temple. Public domain, via Wikimedia Commons.

Figure 12 Titled, "*nittensuishu*" (入鄽垂手, Entering the City with Bliss-bestowing Hands). Postcard, Courtesy of Jotenkaku Museum, Shōkokuji temple. Public domain, via Wikimedia Commons.

are three modes or aspects of the true self.[13] The eighth picture, as I said, is an empty circle. This is where both the ox and the man are gone, which represents that the self has become selfless. And Ueda says that this means that one has opened up to the infinite openness (*kagirinai hirake* 限りない開け).[14] So here, we're no longer in the world in the usual sense. This doesn't mean that we've gone somewhere else. It means that the meanings and values that we're normally engaged with in this world are somehow relativized. They don't have the same weight that they used to have. But what is interesting is that the series doesn't end with the eighth picture where one has become completely selfless, open to infinite openness. Rather, importantly, it depicts how this selfless self *returns to the world* after realizing the "selflessness of the self." This is what we see in the ninth and tenth pictures. Let me briefly comment on the phrase, "selflessness of the self" (*jiko narazaru jiko* 自己ならざる自己). Whereas the eighth picture depicts pure selflessness, he says that the ninth and tenth pictures depict the selflessness of the self but with emphasis placed on different parts. In the ninth picture, the emphasis is put on the *selfless* part of the selfless self, whereas in the tenth picture, it is put on the *self* aspect.[15] Once I explain in more depth what the ninth and tenth pictures talk about, I think what he means by this will become a bit clearer.

So, the ninth picture shows a tree in bloom alongside a river and there is a poem accompanying it that reads the following: *Hana wa onozukara kurenai, mizu wa onozukara boubou* (花は自ずから紅、水は自ずから茫々). There are various translations of this, and some would translate it as: the flowers are red, water flows tranquility. But this doesn't directly translate the word that we are focusing on here, which is *onozukara*. John Maraldo, a scholar on Japanese philosophy, provides the following version in a translation of Ueda's essay: "The flowers blossom just as they blossom [water flows just as it flows]."[16] The word *onozukara* is translated as "just as" here. More literally, one can perhaps translate it as: The flowers blossom naturally of themselves, water flows naturally of itself.

So, we're looking at the ninth picture and the first thing we notice is that no human being is depicted. This means that nature is not seen from *our* perspective because that perspective is completely gone. In other words, nature is not seen as an object. It's not an objectified thing that is standing opposed to us. This is our usual way in which we understand nature, as something that's opposed to the human. But what is depicted in this picture is simply nature. Here, nature is unfolding on its own according to its own way of being and not according to the way we want it to be or understand based on our various ideas and perspectives. And it's important to understand that this is not a metaphor for the true self, but rather, that this is a concrete embodiment of the selflessness of the self.[17] So to be selflessly open *is* to be open to the ways in which things naturally unfold according to their own ways of being. What's interesting is that Ueda uses the word "play" here and says that this is a "selfless play of the self" (自己の「自己ならざる」遊戯).[18] The natural unfolding of things or events is the selfless play of the self.

In Chapter 2, I spoke of the play of nature. The dancing leaves were nature playing. It was playing "in me." But this "me" was not the usual self that is mostly oblivious to nature because of being preoccupied with other things. It was the self that has been cut open by the play of nature. So, the play of nature manifests when there is a selfless play of the self. This is an important point. We're looking at this picture that depicts nature. But what is really being expressed here is not just nature, but what it means to be a self in its selflessness. When one has truly become selfless and become selflessly open, then things naturally unfold according to their own way of being. So, we're not just talking about nature here. We're also talking about what it means for the self to be truly open.

In Chapter 3, I mentioned how Nishida talks about being selflessly present to the flower. He said, "I'm seeing a flower. In this moment, I am the flower, and the flower is me."[19] As I indicated then, this is not to be understood as a metaphor. Rather, we should take this quite seriously. When one is selflessly present to the flower, it doesn't make sense anymore to speak of the flower existing separately from the self. There is really a sense in which you experience yourself as the flower. Nishida also often says that one "becomes the thing" (*mono to naru*, 物となる). One of the recurring lines in his later works is, "seeing by becoming the thing, acting by becoming the thing" (*mono to natte miru, mono to natte okonau*, 物となって見、物となって行う). In fact, in one of the essays, he identifies this as a characteristic feature of Japanese culture.[20] This idea of "becoming the thing" is very much in the spirit of being open to the way things naturally unfold, each according to its own way of being. In Chapter 3, I also mentioned a famous phrase from Matsuo Bashō: from the pine tree learn of the pine tree and from the bamboo of the bamboo (*matsu no koto wa matsu ni narae, take no koto wa take ni narae*, 松のことは松に習え、竹のことは竹に習え). In order to truly understand the pine tree, we need to let go of trying to grasp the pine tree from this and that perspective and become the pine tree itself.

Nishitani Keiji calls the mode of being of the things as they are in themselves, *jōzai* (定在) or samadhi-being.[21] Samadhi is the Buddhist term for the state of the mind that is concentrated on a thing. Here, Nishitani is taking a term that usually applies to the mind and applying it to things to designate their mode of being. Samadhi-being refers to the mode of being of things as they are settled into their own positions. And this can only be achieved in what Nishitani calls the standpoint of sunyata or emptiness. The mind must become empty to let things settle in their home-ground. I like this imagery a lot. The ninth picture shows that things are settled in their own places, following their own ways of unfolding. The mind too is settled. It contrasts nicely to the first picture where the man is looking lost.

Here, I'd like to introduce a poem that Ueda refers to in the context of discussing this ninth picture. It is a poem by the seventeenth-century German mystic and poet, Angelus Silesius:

> The rose is without why
> It blossoms because it blossoms
> To itself it pays no heed
> Asked not if it is seen.[22]

Ueda mentions an episode about Tsujimura Koichi (辻村公一 1922–2010) who is well known today as a famous Heidegger scholar. He's also famous for translating Heidegger's works into Japanese. Tsujimura was studying under Heidegger in Freiburg, and he showed the Oxherding pictures to Heidegger. Heidegger was apparently very impressed, especially with the ninth picture and the poem that accompanies it and said that it is very similar to Angelus Silesius' poem, "Without Why." After mentioning this episode, Ueda goes on to say that although they are very similar, there is a decisive difference between the two, specifically between the "because" in Silesius' poem and the "*onozukara*" in the ninth picture. In Zen Buddhism, he says the negative expression "without why?" is radicalized to the point of infinite nothingness. There is no one asking why and seeking answers. The negative expression corresponds to the eighth picture of the empty circle. The positive expression in Silesius' poem is, "it blossoms because it blossoms." Ueda says that the positive expression in Zen is simplified to a straightforward, "the flowers blossom just as they blossom" in the ninth picture. It's simple in the sense that it is prior to giving reasons and prior to any reflection on its ground. In Silesius' poem, it's still caught up in thought, even though it's not really giving an answer. It's still attempting to give some kind of reason.[23]

Here, Ueda interestingly refers to Heidegger who brings up "play" in this context. Heraclitus famously said, "Lifetime or aion is a child at play moving pieces in a game." Referring to Heraclitus, Heidegger says, "Why does it play, the great child of the world-play that Heraclitus brought into view in the *αἰών*? It plays, because it plays. The 'because' withers away in the play. The play is without 'why.'"[24] Ueda takes note of this but says that a better expression of it is to drop the "because" and to say, "it plays *just as* it plays." He says that if play is really without why, then all references to "because" should be dropped. Otherwise, we'd still be caught up in thinking, a search for reasons. So, the Zen rendering of this is to drop the "because" and to simply say, "it plays just as it plays."[25] So then what we've got here is a contrast between play that is without why and the play of *onozukara* or play understood as a natural unfolding according to its own way of being. I think this is an interesting contrast, something that is worth looking into in more depth. In the Euro-American context, play is typically understood as an activity that has its purpose solely within itself. In our everyday dealings, most of our activities have some sort of purpose outside of itself. We exercise in order to stay healthy, work in order to make our ends meet, sleep in order to have enough energy to work, etc. Play, however, is different. There is no real answer to the question, "why play?" because the purpose of play is to play. When you play, you play not because of this or that reason, not in order to achieve this and that goal, but because it is enjoyable in itself. So, play is without why. But what we've got here is a Zen-inspired understanding of play as play that has dropped all reference to reason and thought, play that comes prior to reflection and thinking. Play in this sense is a natural unfolding of events according to their own ways of being. When I speak of the play of reality or the play of nature, it is this sense of play. Perhaps in attempting to understand play, we've been making it more rational than it actually is when we actually *experience* play. The Zen understanding of play may give us some important insight into the nature of play when we play prior to thinking about play.

So, we've been looking at this *onozukara* way of being that Ueda talks about, a natural unfolding of events according to their own ways of being. *But what does this really mean? What does it mean concretely for things to naturally unfold according to their own ways of being?* What is missing is a phenomenological description that would allow us to get a better understanding of this phenomenon. Recently, together with Erol Čopelj, a friend and colleague of mine, I wrote a paper where we attempted a phenomenological analysis of the *onozukara* way of being.[26] I want to talk about this paper a bit here because I think it might help us get a better grounding of this phenomena in our own experience, rather than just having an idea of what Ueda is talking about.

In our paper, we contrast the *onozukara* way of being to what Martin Heidegger calls our everyday average way of being in the world. According to Heidegger, our basic existence is characterized by what he calls, being-in-the-world. Our particular ways of being, such as being an artist, are all founded on the fact that we always already find ourselves in this world. And to be in the world means to be open to a particular kind of possibility, called projects. Projects are those for the sake of which we engage in our activities. For example, let's say I am working in my own studio with my canvas in order to complete a painting of the mountains that I see from my window. All of this I do for the sake of being an artist. So being an artist is my project. And this means that various possibilities are open to me, such as the possibility of picking up the brush and painting on the canvas, the possibility of seeing the mountains in a specific way, etc.

All of these possibilities are open in virtue of the project of being an artist. Heidegger suggests that while not all of us are artists, all of us exist for the sake of something. As long as we're in this world, we are engaging in some kind of project. And these projects don't have to be something that we consciously take up. Heidegger's point is that regardless of whether we're conscious of them or not, as long as we are in this world, we are engaged in some kind of project. So, Heidegger seems to be suggesting that we necessarily exist for the sake of something. But this would mean the only possibilities that are available to us in this world are those that are brought about by our projects. Now, this idea seems to miss a deeper kind of possibility that is present in the world. And this is something that we can see everywhere in nature.

Say that a farmer is cultivating crops. The possibility of cultivating crops is open to him in virtue of his project of being a farmer. But that possibility wouldn't have been open in the first place if it weren't for the possibility for the plant to grow and to give some kind of fruit. And that possibility is not *our* possibility, it's not the kind of possibility that's brought about by our projects. It is rather something intrinsic to the plant. This kind of possibility is not only present in nature, but in fact it's everywhere. Any transition that we see in this world is actually an example of this kind of possibility. Not *our* possibility, but the possibility that pertains to the things themselves. We call this kind of possibility "thingly possibility" and it's an idea that Erol developed in detail in his PhD dissertation[27] and his new book that just recently came out.[28]

Now, in order to clarify the presence of this other kind of possibility, thingly possibility, we focus on the transition from our everyday average way of being in the world, which Heidegger calls "inauthenticity," to when this breaks down in anxiety. The reason why we focus on this specific transition is because it's a sort of violent transition that allows us to become aware of this other kind of possibility that is otherwise covered up by our possibilities and projects. I won't go into the detail of the analysis that we undertake in our paper. It involves engaging with Heidegger's analysis in *Being and Time* and it's not really important for our purposes here. But the main idea is that although Heidegger didn't really pay attention to the transition from inauthenticity to anxiety, a close look at it reveals that we can't really make sense of this transition solely in terms of *our* possibility. It is an example of what we call thingly possibility. It pertains to the intrinsic possibility of our being that at times we break down into anxiety. This possibility is not something that we primarily bring about, even though in a rather weird case, one could engage in a project to deliberately bring about the anxious state.

We can take a look at an example of a flowing stream to contrast these two kinds of possibilities, projects and thingly possibilities. A flowing stream is necessarily open towards the future. There's a futural dimension to a flowing stream. But there are two ways in which we can understand this openness towards the future. One is based on our projects. So, say that I have a project of taking a photo of the stream. It's a beautiful stream and I want to capture it on my camera so that I can share it on my Instagram. So, the bigger project at work here may be gaining recognition from others.

Now, this project opens up various possibilities for me. The stream affords me the possibility of being captured on camera, the sun has the possibility of providing enough light and so on. These possibilities are open in virtue of having the project. But the stream is also open to the future in another sense. The stream is constantly changing over time and it's constantly renewing itself. There's a new arrangement of color and shades every moment and no two moments are the same. This kind of possibility is intrinsic to the flowing stream. It pertains to the thingly possibility of the stream. If we contrast the project of taking a photo to the thingly possibility of the flowing stream, we see that in my project of taking a photo, there's a *grasping* of the phenomena. I want this stream and the lighting to be a certain way so that I can take a good picture which is going to gain a lot of views on Instagram.

So, projects are accompanied by a grasping and a *controlling* of the phenomena. If the weather changes and it gets cloudy all of a sudden, I will be disappointed and most likely lose interest in the stream. This is quite different from the way we relate to thingly possibilities. Rather than trying to grasp and control the phenomena, we relate to thingly possibilities by *tuning in* to the phenomenon. Instead of trying to make things a specific way, we *listen* to the ways in which the phenomenon is unfolding. Instead of the disappointment from failing to live up to my expectations, there is rather an appreciation accompanied by surprise and wonder for the way in which the thing unfolds towards its own future. So, whereas projects have a for-the-sake-of-which structure, thingly possibilities have an unfolding-towards structure. Things necessarily unfold towards a specific future, a future that is not projected by us, but is decided by the things themselves.

This is just a snapshot of what we do in our paper. But the main reason for bringing this up here is because I think it may help us get a better grip on the *onozukara* way of being. What we've called thingly possibilities is precisely the *onozukara* way of being that pertains, not just to nature, but to any kind of thing. In order to understand things as they unfold according to their own nature, we need to *tune out* of our projects and *tune in* to the thingly possibilities. And we too have our own thingly possibility that we need to listen to since most of the time we're *not* in tune with it. A good indication that you may not be in tune is when you're putting a lot of effort trying to make things a particular way, a way that is imposed from without, based on our projects.

This manifests in our body too. As we mentioned before in Chapter 7, when we're defending a position, our body becomes rigid. Instead of engaging in a discussion with open ears, we try to prove that we're right and put a lot of energy in that. If we can let go of that grasping even just a bit, that's already a great start. But it's important to note that listening and tuning in also requires some effort on our part. It's not the same as just relaxing and doing nothing. The effort that is required here, however, has a very different feel from the effort you put in when you're trying to make things go your way. These observations are coming from my own experience, and they are, of course, for our readers to check for themselves.

Finally, I want to talk about the last picture of the Ten Oxherding pictures. As I said in the beginning, the eighth picture, according to Ueda, depicts selflessness, how the self has become selfless, whereas the ninth and the tenth pictures represent how the selfless self manifests in the world, how one returns to the world after realizing the selflessness. And we said that the ninth picture puts emphasis on the "selfless" aspect of the "selfless self" whereas in the tenth picture, the emphasis is put on the "self" of the "selfless self." Referring to the difference between *onozukara* and *mizukara*, we could perhaps say that the ninth picture is talking about the *onozukara* aspect, how things naturally occur of themselves, while the tenth picture is referring to the *mizukara* aspect, how something is done by oneself, the personal initiative aspect.

The tenth picture gives us some important insight into what a true encounter between people might look like. In the picture, you see two people that seem to be exchanging something. The first thing Ueda says is that the true self is *not* represented as either the old one or the younger one. Rather, the true self is the *two people meeting and facing each other*. The true self is *both* the self and the other. Put differently, the self has opened up to the in-between of the self and other. Or rather, he says the in-between has been "cut open."[29] So the key word here is the "between" or the "in-between" or *aida* or *ma* (間) in Japanese which is one of the characters in the Japanese word for human being or person, *ningen* (人間). Ueda says the true self is the *ningen*, putting emphasis on the second character, *aida*. So the true self is the "between of the persons." What exactly does he mean by this?

Before we look into this further, I think it might be worth saying a few words about this concept of *aida* or *ma*, which is an important concept in Japanese thought. This concept is omnipresent in Japanese culture. It is an important concept in everyday speech, for example. One person speaks and before the other responds, there is silence. This *ma* is not an awkward silence waiting to be filled. It is the space that gives room for others to contemplate before talking. *Ma* is also an important concept in Japanese aesthetics. In traditional ink paintings you see a lot of empty space, and this has as much an important role as the actual painting. There are many paintings where there's much more empty space than the actual thing that is depicted. In martial arts, too, they say it is important to understand the *maai* (間合い) which is the space between the competitors.

Going back to the word *ningen*. . .The word is comprised of two characters, *nin* (人) and *gen* (間). *Nin* (人) means "human" or "person" and *gen* (間) means "between" or "space." So just looking at the characters, the word suggests that human beings are not isolated, individual beings, but are fundamentally relational. Watsuji Tetsurō (和辻哲郎, 1889–1960), who is usually counted as one of the Kyoto School members and who wrote on Japanese ethics, analyzes this word *ningen*. And he talks about how *ningen* initially didn't mean individual human beings, but that it stood for *seken* (世間) which means society or the public and only later came to signify people. He then goes on to say how humans are not only individual beings, but also social beings. We have this kind of dual nature. We are *aidagara teki sonzai* (間柄的存在) which can be translated as relational beings.[30] The second character of *aidagara* (間柄) means pattern. So, one could translate *aidagara* to mean patterns of betweenness or patterns of interpersonal relationships.

So, with this idea of relational beings, Watsuji wanted to say that we're not first individuals that then enter into relations with other people, but rather, we're first and foremost relational beings. We are who we are in relation to other people. We find ourselves in different patterns of relationality, whether that's family, colleagues, friends ... and all of those relationalities are what defines who we are.[31] Watsuji's analysis of the Japanese conception of human beings I think still holds today. Japanese society emphasizes the relationship between people and tends to prioritize that over what is good for the individual. There are both good and bad sides to this, but it is a tendency that you can observe everywhere from school, workplace, to various organizations.

Now, when Ueda focuses on this concept of *aida* in *ningen* and claims that the true self is the between of the self and other, what does he really mean by that? Is he echoing Watsuji and saying that we should understand ourselves as relational beings? I think that he seems to be saying something a bit more than that. And I think we can find some hints to understanding this in his analysis of the famous Zen dialogue in the *Blue Cliff Record*, case 68. It's a dialogue between two masters Kyōsan Ejaku (仰山慧寂) and Sanshō Enen (三聖慧然) and he raises this as an example of what in the Zen tradition is called *hinju gokan* (賓主互換) or mutual exchange of host and guest.[32] *Hin* (賓) is guest and *ju* or *shu* (主) is host or master.

The dialogue is very short:

Kyōsan Ejaku asked Sanshō Enen, "What is your name?"
Sanshō said "Ejaku!"
Ejaku replied, "Kyōsan, that's my name!"
"Well then," said Sanshō, "My name is Enen."
Kyōsan roared with laughter.

As with many Zen dialogues, this one is also quite puzzling. You don't really know what's going on at first glance. It even seems like some sort of a joke. But according to Ueda, this exemplifies what the mutual exchange of host and guest is about in its ultimate form. In the first line, Kyōsan is expressing his authority and mastery by asking for Sanshō's name. Even today when someone asks for another's name, this is a sign of authority, like a police officer asking for a person's name. Now, Kyōsan knows Sanshō very well, so he is not really asking for his name. It's rather a kind of test. Instead of giving his own name and submitting to Kyōsan's authority, Sanshō reclaims his autonomy by replying with Kyōsan's name. He is saying that he too is a master, that he too is a host. Then, when Kyōsan replies that is my name, he is not really surrendering to Sanshō, but rather he's accepting the invitation and voluntarily becoming the guest. And Sanshō does the same when he finally gives his own name. So, the dialogue, although very short, demonstrates how the two masters playfully but also in a combative way exchange the roles of host and guest.

I find this idea of the mutual exchange of host and guest very interesting, and I think this is one way we can understand what Ueda means when he says that the true self is the between of the self and other. Maybe this becomes less abstract if we understand this between as a dynamic space where this exchange of roles takes place. Perhaps Ueda is saying that the true self is one that can playfully exchange this role of host and guest. Host and guest here can be understood in several ways, but I think an important aspect of being a host is saying "I" and speaking your voice, while being the guest would mean letting the other speak and becoming the listener.

Yamada Mumon (山田無文, 1900–1988), a Rinzai Rōshi and a former head of the Myōshinji temple in Kyoto, nicely sums up what this mutual exchange is about. He says, "I am you and you are me. If you say you don't get that kind of state, then you don't get Rinzai Zen" (*ore ga omae de omae ga ore da. Souiu kyochi ga wakarantoiuto Rinzai Zen wa wakaran* 俺がおまえで、おまえが俺だ。そういう境地が分からんというと、臨済禅は分からん).[33] What can't be captured in the English translation is that the first and second personal pronouns he uses, "*ore*" for me and "*omae*" for you, are very casual and rather rough. I find it quite funny that a Zen Rōshi is speaking in this way. But it also makes it more familiar and real. In any case, this way of putting it is very similar to what Nishida says about the flower: "I am the flower, the flower is me." They are essentially expressing the same thing. The difference is that here it is about people.

So, the last picture is about how one comes back to the self and says "I" after realizing the selflessness. Ueda seems to be suggesting that this self is not a fixed self, but a self that can enter into a dynamic relationship with other people. And dynamic in a quite radical sense. Not just relating to other people in various relationships and understanding yourself in relation to other people, but changing roles with other people. We speak of trying to stand in the other's shoes in order to understand the other person. The mutual exchange of host and guest is more than just standing in the other's shoes. It's saying that in order to understand the other person, you really have to *become* that person in ways we've discussed here and in previous chapters.

This is quite radical. If you were already skeptical about the idea of becoming the flower, then this idea of becoming another person would probably strike you as impossible. But is it really impossible? Or does it only seem impossible because you understand this in the ordinary way based on the idea that we are separate selves?

I have found that simply leaving this possibility open and trying it out on various occasions to see how much I can really become another person has been helpful. It's certainly worth experimenting with in your own experiences.

Speaking more generally, such ongoing practice and experimentation have been our main emphasis throughout this book—be open to reality, and *play!*

Discussion Questions

- Chapter 8 begins with a discussion of the central notion of "practice," its importance and link with appreciating impermanence in life. Can you work with that focus in your own life? Does the emphasis on impermanence seem disturbing or enlivening? Does it aid participation, engagement?
- In this chapter, we discussed the possibility of "becoming the thing" and how this involves tuning in to the "thingly possibility" of the particular thing in question. The Japanese word for "thing" is "*mono*" (もの、物) which stands for things in general and it is the same word in "*mono no aware*." How do you think "*mono*" differs from "objects" (which would be "*taishō*" (対象) or "*kyakutai*" (客体) in Japanese)? Why would "objects" be inappropriate here?
- Towards the end it was mentioned that the "mutual exchange of host and guest" is more radical than standing in another person's shoes because it involves "becoming the other person." When you usually try to stand in another's shoes, what do you think prevents you from "becoming the other person"? Can you try to bracket some of those things, and what happens as a result?

Recommended Readings

If you are interested in learning more about phenomenology, Japanese philosophy, and some of the contemplative traditions dealt with in this book, below is a list of selected introductory texts and supplementary materials with a brief explanation about each text.

Phenomenology

Dan Zahavi, *Phenomenology: The Basics*. Abingdon: Routledge, 2019.

If you are looking for a short, accessible but also reliable introduction to phenomenology, this is the book for you. Written by one of the leading scholars on phenomenology, the book covers the key concepts that are necessary for understanding phenomenology and deals with some of its practical applications in sociology, psychology and other disciplines.

Dermot Moran, *Introduction to Phenomenology*. London: Routledge, 2000.

This book is a comprehensive guide to the phenomenological movement starting with its origins in Husserl and going through some of the most famous phenomenologists such as Heidegger, Sartre, and Merleau-Ponty as well as the lesser-known figures such as Levinas, Arendt, and Gadamer. A great introductory book for anyone who wants an overview of the phenomenological movement.

Phenomenological Epoché

Dan Zahavi, *Husserl's Phenomenology*. Stanford: Stanford University Press, 2003. See Chapter 2: "Husserl's turn to transcendental philosophy: epoché, reduction, and transcendental idealism."

In this book, which is one of the most popular and accessible introductory books on Husserl's phenomenology, the author provides a concise and clear explanation of the phenomenological epoché and the reduction and their differences. This will give you a good understanding of why and for what purpose Husserl originally introduced the epoché.

William Jon Lenkowski, "What is Husserl's epoché?: the problem of the beginning of philosophy in a Husserlian context," *Man and World* 11 (1978): 299–323.

Written by a relatively unknown author, this article was one of the most insightful and inspiring articles for me (Yuko) while working on this book project. The author argues that the epoché, which marks the beginning of philosophy in anyone is initially not something that we actively bring about, as Husserl had thought, but is something that happens to us. We "fall into perplexity" and the sustaining of this fall, according to the author, is what we do with the epoché.

Kyoto School Tradition and Japanese Philosophy

Robert E. Carter, *Kyoto School: An Introduction*. Albany: SUNY Press, 2013.

This is a great introductory book to the Kyoto School philosophy written by an eminent philosopher and ethicist who has long been working on modern and traditional Japanese thought. It deals with the philosophy of Nishida Kitarō, Tanabe Hajime, Nishitani Keiji, and Watsuji Tetsurō, four of the key thinkers in the Kyoto School tradition. The book makes their ideas accessible and relatable, and it is written in a way that invites the reader to explore further.

Thomas P. Kasulis, *Engaging Japanese Philosophy: A Short History*. Honolulu: University of Hawaii Press, 2018.

This book, which is almost 800 pages long, is written by a renowned scholar on Japanese religious thought and covers a wide range of philosophical and religious thinkers and ideas from ancient to medieval and modern history of Japan including Kūkai, Shinran, Dōgen, Motoori Norinaga, and Nishida Kitarō and Watsuji Tetsurō from the Kyoto School tradition. What is great about this book is its breadth and how he guides the reader to engage with each thinker through various analogies, examples and thought experiments.

Buddhism

Many popular-level books are available on basic aspects of Buddhism and introductory practices, and the reader is encouraged to browse and settle on what seems accessible and interesting to get started. (For introductory practice books, see the Japanese Zen section below.) Here are three that give glimpses of Buddhism's more technical, theoretical side and its views regarding ethics.

Herbert V. Guenther, *Buddhist Philosophy in Theory and Practice*. Baltimore: Penguin Books, 1972.

Guenther's book offers a useful comparison of several Buddhist philosophical schools, as summarized in two traditional Tibetan texts. Readers will need cross-reading with other sources to fully understand some of its points, but the book is cited because it deals with issues also related to modern phenomenology. This book is no longer in print, but copies are still available.

Georges B. J. Dreyfus, *Recognizing Reality: Dharmakirti's Philosophy and its Tibetan Interpretations.* Albany: SUNY Press, 1997.

An example of how Buddhist philosophers in India and Tibet used serious consideration and debate of epistemological points as a support for—and even a supplementary inroad to—Buddhist contemplative practice. It discusses the interaction between realist (materialist) and anti-realist or idealist positions held within the larger institution of Buddhism. It's very technical, but a possible sourcebook for students interested in how Buddhism has tackled philosophical issues common to both European and Asian cultures.

Hammalawa Saddhatissa, *Buddhist Ethics.* Somerville: Wisdom Publications, 1997.

An informed but non-technical presentation of the historical context and actual practice of Buddhist Ethics. Considers how both monastic and lay-practitioners understand and apply Buddhist ethical commitments.

Japanese Zen

Shunryu Suzuki, *Zen Mind, Beginner's Mind: Informal Talks on Zen Meditation and Practice.* New York and Tokyo: John Weatherhill, 1989.

As the title implies, this is a set of edited talks given by Shunryu Suzuki, Rōshi to some students in California. Seemingly simple, informal comments on the fundamentals of Zen practice related to the Sōtō school founded by Dōgen Zenji.

Dainin Katagiri, *Returning to Silence: Zen Practice in Daily Life.* Boston: Shambala Publications, 1988.

An accessible and useful expansion on points raised in *Zen Mind, Beginner's Mind.* Karagiri was a successor to Suzuki Rōshi, and had extensive experience teaching lay-people.

Daoism

The best-known text associated with Daoism is the Daodeching, an early exposition of the "Dao" or Way. There are many translations into English, which have their various virtues. Two are listed below.

Ellen M. Chen, *The Tao Te Ching: A New Translation with Commentary.* New York: Paragon House, 1989.

One of the more technically accurate renderings, with useful commentaries on the main point of each chapter and discussions of specific interpretive challenges and translation choices.

Red Pine (Bill Porter), *Lao-Tzu's Taoteching.* San Francisco: Mercury House, 1996.

An English translation with the Chinese (Mandarin) characters set alongside. Each chapter is supplemented by explanatory, historically interesting, and sometimes quirky quotations from Chinese authors representing various traditions or positions.

Confucianism

David L. Hall and Roger T. Ames, *Thinking Through Confucius.* Albany: SUNY Press, 1987.

A cultivation-oriented approach to Confucian teachings, based on analyses of the main Chinese characters used in classic Confucian texts.

Tu Wei-ming, *Confucian Thought: Selfhood as Creative Transformation.* Albany: SUNY Press, 1985.

Essays on Confucian views of the "human way" and significance of personhood in the context of community. A starting point for considering more detailed works on Confucian theory.

Notes

1 An Invitation to Play with Reality

1. Edmund Husserl, *Ideas Pertaining to a Pure Phenomenology and to a Phenomenological Philosophy: First Book*, trans. Fred Kersten (The Hague: Martinus Nijhoff, 1983), § 31.
2. In Chapter 6, we discuss the different ways that phenomenology has been practiced since Husserl, including its application outside of philosophy such as psychology and psychiatry. We mention that the epoché may not be necessary in such cases given how technical the epoché is.

2 Falling into Play

1. This idea of "spontaneously falling into the play of reality" was inspired by William J. Lenkowski's article, "What is Husserl's epoché?". For Husserl, a philosopher first becomes a philosopher by executing the epoché. So how does this epoché come to be performed? Husserl's answer to this question was that it is within his freedom to do so and that one must resolve to become a philosopher since no one simply falls into philosophy. Against this idea, which sounds overly voluntarist, Lenkowski proposes that the epoché is primarily something that we fall into. William J. Lenkowski, "What is Husserl's epoché? The problem of the beginning of philosophy in a Husserlian context," *Man and World* 11 (1978): 299–323.
2. This idea of the "play of reality," that reality is a kind of play, is reminiscent of the idea of "world-play" we find in the history of philosophy. Heraclitus, for example, famously said that lifetime (*αἰών*) is a child at play, playing draughts; to the kingship is a child's (Fragment 52). In the phenomenological tradition, Eugen Fink (1905–1975), who was Husserl's assistant in his later years, wrote extensively on the topic of play and developed the idea that the world is itself a play and that we humans are co-players in this play of the world. I do not engage with Fink's discussion in this book, however, because it is very much metaphysical and offers little insight into the practice of play. Eugen Fink, *Play as the Symbol of the World*, trans. Ian Alexander Moore and Christopher Turner (Bloomington and Indianapolis: Indiana University Press, 2016). The third-generation Kyoto School philosopher, Ueda Shizuteru, also speaks of the "world-play" (*sekai yūgi* 世界遊戲) in the context of developing his idea of the "twofold-being-in-the-world" (*nijyū sekai nai sonzai* 二重世界内存在). While Ueda's discussion is less theoretical, I do not refer to it in this book because it requires engaging with his philosophy in

some detail, which is beyond our purposes here. Shizuteru Ueda, *Ueda Shizuteru Shū* Vol. 9 (*Kokū/Sekai* [Open Expanse/World]) (Tokyo: Iwanami Shoten, 2002), Part I, Chapter 5: "*Sekai yūgi to nijyū sekai nai sonzai*" (「世界遊戯と二重世界内存在」).

3 Perhaps we can make an analogy here to how we go from being a novice to becoming skilled in some activity. As a novice, you are conscious of all your bodily movements and there is a clear sense of you trying to control the situation and the activity. But as you get more skilled, there is a sense in which this "you" fades into the background and the activity flows on its own. In his maiden work, *Zen no kenkyū* (『善の研究』, 1911, translated into English under the title, *An Inquiry into the Good*), Nishida Kitarō called this kind of heightened activity, "pure experience" (*junsui keiken* 純粋経験). He provides a few examples of pure experience from skilled performance such as climbing a cliff and an expert musician playing music. He also speaks of how the painter's brush moves spontaneously when inspiration arises in him. Kitarō Nishida, *An Inquiry into the Good*, trans. Masao Abe and Christopher Ives (New Haven, CT and London: Yale University Press, 1990), 6; 32.

4 Some have noted similarities between the phenomenological epoché and aesthetic detachment. See, for example: Rudolf Bernet, "Phenomenological and aesthetic *epoché*: painting the invisible things themselves," in *The Oxford Handbook of Contemporary Phenomenology*, ed. Dan Zahavi (Oxford: Oxford University Press, 2012), 564–582. In fact, as Bernet mentions in the article, Husserl himself compared the attitude of the phenomenologist to that of the artist in a letter to the Austrian poet, Hugo von Hofmannsthal. Bernet writes: "Both the phenomenologist and the artist consider things, persons, events, and the entire world from a distance and with wonder. Compared to ordinary people (or with themselves in ordinary life), phenomenologists and artists have both lost and gained something at the same time. What they have lost is their familiarity with the surrounding world, their spontaneous understanding of the meanings of things, and their capacity to immediately see what needs to be done in all circumstances of practical life. What they have gained is a perception of the world freed from the need of orientation, a non-instrumental relation to things, and a consideration of worldly events and situations for their own sake. Phenomenological and artistic perceivers have thus exchanged their own know-how about things and their knowledge of the world for the discovery of the coming forth or 'birth' of both things and the world out of a manifold of ever changing appearances" (p. 567).

3 Openness, Playfulness, and Freedom

1 Husserl articulates the "principle of all principles" in the *Ideas I* as follows: "*[E]very originary presentative intuition is a legitimizing source of cognition* [. . .] *everything originarily* (so to speak, in its 'personal' actuality) *offered* to us

in 'intuition' is to be accepted simply as what it is presented as being, but also *only within the limits in which it is presented there.*" Husserl, *Ideas: First Book*, 44.

2 Husserl, *Ideas: First Book*, 60–62.

3 Jean-Paul Sartre, *The Imaginary: A Phenomenological Psychology of the Imagination*, trans. Jonathan Webber (London and New York: Routledge, 2004), 14.

4 Hans-Georg Gadamer, *Truth and Method*, trans. Joel Weinsheimer and Donald G. Marsh (London and New York: Continuum, 2004), 273.

5 Gadamer, *Truth and Method*, 268–273.

6 Gadamer introduces the concept of play in *Truth and Method* in his discussion of our experience of art and what is involved in understanding artworks. In contrast to the idea that the meaning of an artwork exists somewhere hidden within the artwork and independently of the spectator, Gadamer tries to show that an artwork's meaning is revealed "in-between" the artwork and the spectators, in the back-and-forth movement of presentation and recognition. Towards the end of the discussion, he attempts to generalize the idea of the play of understanding in artworks to understanding texts of all kinds. Gadamer, *Truth and Method*, 153–161. For an insightful discussion of Gadamer's idea of the play of understanding, see: Monica Vilhauer, *Gadamer's Ethics of Play: Hermeneutics and the Other* (Plymouth: Lexington Books, 2010).

7 Gadamer says: "[A]ll playing is a being played. The attraction of a game, the fascination it exerts, consists precisely in the fact that the game masters the players. Even in the case of games in which one tries to perform tasks that one has set oneself, there is a risk that they will not 'work,' 'succeed,' or 'succeed again,' which is the attraction of the game. Whoever 'tries' is in fact the one who is tried. The real subject of the game (this is shown in precisely those experiences in which there is only a single player) is not the player but instead the game itself. What holds the player in its spell, draws him into play, and keeps him there is the game itself." Gadamer, *Truth and Method*, 106.

8 Paul Ricoeur, "Appropriation," in *Hermeneutics and the Human Sciences: Essays on Language, Action and Interpretation*, ed. and trans. John B. Thompson (Cambridge: Cambridge University Press, 1981).

9 Ricoeur, "Appropriation," 153.

10 Ricoeur, "Appropriation," 147.

11 For example, he says: "Hermeneutical distanciation is not unrelated to the phenomenological *epoché*, that is, to an *epoché* interpreted in a non-idealist sense as an aspect of the intentional movement of consciousness towards meaning. For all consciousness of meaning involves a moment of distanciation, a distancing from 'lived experience' as purely and simply adhered to. Phenomenology begins when, not content to 'live' or 'relive,' we interrupt lived experience in order to signify it. Thus the *epoché* and the meaning-intention are closely linked." Paul Ricoeur, "Phenomenology and hermeneutics," in *Hermeneutics and the Human Sciences: Essays on Language,*

Action and Interpretation, ed. and trans. John B. Thompson (Cambridge: Cambridge University Press, 1981), 76. For an interesting article that examines the connection between Husserl's epoché and Ricoeur's notion of distanciation, see: Leslie MacAvoy, "Distanciation and *epoché*: the influence of Husserl on Ricoeur's hermeneutics," in *Hermeneutics and Phenomenology in Paul Ricoeur: Between Text and Phenomenon*, ed. Scott Davidson and Marc-Antoine Vallée (Dordrecht: Springer, 2016), 13–30.

12 Ricoeur, "Appropriation," 153.

13 Ricoeur, "Appropriation," 155.

14 Gadamer, *Truth and Method*, 104.

15 It was not Nishida, but Ueda Shizuteru, a third-generation Kyoto School philosopher, that speaks of the *suspension of reflection*. According to Ueda, Nishida employs philosophical reflection in a radical sense since he takes reflection back to direct experience that is not only *prior to* reflection but is *beyond* it (in the sense that it cannot be grasped reflectively). *But if reflection cannot disclose such a direct experience, how is it possible to take reflection back to such an experience?* "Suspension of reflection" is Ueda's answer to this question. By bracketing the reflecting "I," it prepares one to encounter reality beyond reflection. While it is comparable to Husserl's phenomenological epoché, Ueda says that it is also much more radical: "While the suspension of judgment is a specific method of philosophical reflection, the suspension of reflection [*hansei teishi* 反省停止] is a way of reflecting on the practice of philosophy itself." It is radical because it questions the very belief in reflection. Shizuteru Ueda, *Ueda Shizuteru Shū Vol. 2: Keiken to jikaku* (Tokyo: Iwanami Shoten, 2002), 210–211. See also: Yuko Ishihara, "Nishida and Ueda on philosophical reflection," in *Tetsugaku Companion to Ueda Shizuteru: Language, Experience, and Zen* (Series: Tetsugaku Companions to Japanese Philosophy), ed. Raquel Bouso et al. (Cham: Springer, 2022).

16 Ueda mentions that suspension of reflection is essentially a "practice" (*gyō* 行). It is not something that we can just do by thinking about it, but requires one to actually attempt putting aside the reflecting "I" and see what is offered to us in our experience. It is a practice in the sense that it requires engagement, exploration, and diligence. See Chapter 8 for more discussion on "practice" as "*gyō*" (行) in the Japanese tradition.

17 Nishida's idea of pure experience (*junsui keiken* 純粋経験) is first presented in his maiden work, *Zen no kenkyū* (『善の研究』), first published in 1911 (the English translation is titled, *An Inquiry into the Good*).

18 The original reads: *Ware hana o miru. Kono toki hana wa ware, ware wa hana dearu* (我花を見る。此時花は我、我は花である). Nishida provides this example of the flower in his early, posthumously published writing, "Fragmentary notes on pure experience" (「純粋経験に関する断章」). While the exact years these notes were written are unknown, they were supposedly composed around the time *An Inquiry into the Good* was originally published in 1911. Kitarō Nishida, "*Junsuikeiken ni kansuru danshō*"

[Fragmentary notes on pure experience], in *Nishida Kitarō Zenshū* Vol. 16 (*Shoki sōkō [Early Writings]*), ed. Yoshishige Abe et al. (Tokyo: Iwanami Shoten, 1980), 430.

19 The famous phrase appears in the *Akasōshi* (赤冊子, meaning "red booklet") compiled in *Sanzōshi* (三冊子, meaning "three booklets"). *Sanzōshi* is a collection of notes on Bashō's ideas on poetry written by Bashō's disciple, Hattori Tohō (服部土芳 1657–1730). Taizō Ebara, ed. *Kyoraishō, Sanzōshi, Tabineron* (Tokyo: Iwanami Shoten, 1993), 101.

20 Kitarō Nishida, "*Nihon bunka no mondai*" [The problems of Japanese culture], in *Nishida Kitarō Zenshū* Vol. 12, ed. Yoshishige Abe et al. (Tokyo: Iwanami Shoten, 1979), 346.

21 Keiji Nishitani, "The standpoint of sunyata," in *Religion and Nothingness*, trans. Jan van Bragt (Berkeley: University of California Press, 1982), 119–167.

22 Ebara, *Kyoraishō*, 104.

23 I will discuss more about the Japanese sense of nature in Chapter 8.

4 Practicing Playing

1 We will say more about this as it relates to Kant's transcendental philosophy in Chapter 6.

2 This exercise is an adaptation of one with the same name introduced in *Time, Space & Knowledge: A New Vision of Reality*, by Steven Tainer's teacher, Tarthang Tulku Rinpoche. In our present book the technique is applied in a different way and in the context of phenomenology. Tarthang Tulku, *Time, Space & Knowledge: A New Vision of Reality* (Berkeley: Dharma Publishing, 1977), 258–259.

3 In Chapter 8, I give more examples from the Japanese language and discuss how the language reflects the way Japanese people have traditionally understood the relation between human and nature.

5 A Conversation with Contemplative Traditions

1 What I have here called the "higher sense of play" relates to the Zen understanding of play that I discuss in Chapter 8, Section 3: Interpreting the Ten Oxherding Pictures.

2 On what "practicing phenomenology" meant for Husserl and his successors, and how they differ from what it means to practice phenomenology for us in this book, see Chapter 6.

3 In 1906, for example, he says that his main task as a philosopher is a critique of reason, which was broken down into theoretical, practical, and evaluative

reason. For Husserl, these corresponded to logic, ethics, and axiology. Edmund Husserl, "Beilage IX: Persönliche Aufzeichnungen vom 25.9.1905, 4.11.1907 und 6.3.1908," in *Einleitung in die Logik und Erkenntnistheorie Vorlesungen 1906/07 Husserliana* 24 (Den Haag: Nijhoff, 1984), 442–449.

4 Edmund Husserl, *The Crisis of European Sciences and Transcendental Phenomenology: An Introduction to Phenomenological Philosophy*, trans. David Carr (Evanston: Northwestern University, 1988), 137.

6 Practicing Phenomenology—the Historico-Theoretical Context

1 Dan Zahavi, "Applied phenomenology: why it is safe to ignore the epoché," *Continental Philosophy Review* 54 (2021): 259–273. https://doi.org/10.1007/s11007-019-09463-y.

2 See: Karam Tej Singh Sarao, "Vasubandhu," *The Internet Encyclopedia of Philosophy*, https://iep.utm.edu/vasubandhu/, September 25, 2022; Dan Lusthaus, *Buddhist Phenomenology: A Philosophical Investigation of Yogacara Buddhism and the Ch'eng Wei-shih Lun* (New York: Routledge, 2003); Jonathan C. Gold, "Vasubandhu," *The Stanford Encyclopedia of Philosophy* (Spring 2021 Edition), ed. Edward N. Zalta, https://plato.stanford.edu/archives/spr2021/entries/vasubandhu/; Jan Christoph Westerhoff, "Nāgārjuna," *The Stanford Encyclopedia of Philosophy* (Summer 2022 Edition), ed. Edward N. Zalta, https://plato.stanford.edu/archives/sum2022/entries/nagarjuna/.

3 See: Alison Gopnik, "Could David Hume have known about Buddhism?: Charles François Dolu, the Royal College of La Flèche, and the Global Jesuit Intellectual Network," *Hume Studies* 35, Numbers 1 and 2 (2009): 5–28; Abraham Velez, "Buddha (c. 500s B.C.E)," *The Internet Encyclopedia of Philosophy*, https://iep.utm.edu/buddha/, September 25, 2022. See also: Georges B. J. Dreyfus, *Recognizing Reality: Dharmakirti's Philosophy and its Tibetan Interpretations* (Albany: SUNY Press, 1997).

4 Yuko Ishihara, "Transcendental philosophy and its transformations: Heidegger and Nishida's critical engagements with transcendental philosophy in the late 1920s" (PhD dissertation, University of Copenhagen, 2016).

5 Nishida, *An Inquiry into the Good*, 19.

6 Yuko Ishihara, "Nishida Kitarō's awakened realism: going radically transcendental," *Metodo: International Studies in Phenomenology and Philosophy*, Special Issue 1.3: On the Transcendental (2019): 57–84. https://doi.org/10.19079/metodo.s1.3.57.

7 Practicing Phenomenology—the Personal Side in Practice and "Play"

1 Husserl, *The Crisis of European Sciences and Transcendental Phenomenology*, 137.
2 Edmund Husserl, *On the Phenomenology of the Consciousness of Internal Time (1893–1917)*, ed. and trans. J. B. Brough (Dordrecht: Kluwer, 1991).

8 Japanese Perspectives on "Practice," "Nature," and "Play"

1 Keiji Nishitani, "*Bashō ni tsuite*" [On Bashō], in *Shūkyo to Hishūkyo no aida* [Between Religion and Non-religion], ed. Shizuteru Ueda (Tokyo: Iwanami Shoten, 2001), 134–136.
2 Nishitani, "*Bashō*," 141–145.
3 Nishitani, "*Bashō*," 138.
4 Nishitani, "*Bashō*," 137–140.
5 Nishitani, "*Bashō*," 140–141.
6 Keiji Nishitani, "*Gyō to iu koto*" [To Practice], in *Shūkyo to Hishūkyo no aida* [Between Religion and Non-religion], ed. Shizuteru Ueda (Tokyo: Iwanami Shoten, 2001), 95.
7 Nishitani, "*Gyō*," 95–96.
8 Shizuteru Ueda, *Nishida Kitarō o yomu* [Reading Nishida Kitarō] (Tokyo: Iwanami Shoten, 1991), 234–244.
9 Tim Chilcott, "Matsuo Bashō: *Oku no Hosomichi*, The Narrow Road to the Deep North," *Tim Chilcott Literary Translations*, 2004, 3, http://www.tclt.org.uk/basho/Oku_2011.pdf.
10 Seiichi Takeuchi, *"Onozukara" to "Mizukara": Nihon shisō: no kisō* ["Onozukara" and "Mizukara": The Basis of Japanese Thought] (Tokyo: Shunjyūsha, 2004), 204–208. See also: Seiichi Takeuchi, *Nihonjin wa naze "sayonara" to wakareru noka* [Why Japanese People Say "Sayonara"], Chikuma Shinsho Series (Tokyo: Chikuma Shobō, 2009).
11 Bret W. Davis, "Natural freedom: human/nature non-dualism in Japanese thought," in *The Oxford Handbook of World Philosophy*, ed. Jay Garfield and William Edelglass (New York: Oxford University Press, 2011), 336.
12 Ueda offers a comprehensive analysis of the Ten Oxherding Pictures in: Shizuteru Ueda, *Ueda Shizuteru Shū* Vol. 6 (*Dōtei "Jūgyūzu" o ayumu* [Walking the Passage "Ten Oxherding Pictures"]) (Tokyo: Iwanami Shoten, 2003). Here, I refer to his text in *Ueda Shizuteru Shū* Volume 9, where we can find a concise version of his analysis.
13 Ueda, *Ueda Shizuteru Shū* Vol. 9, 153.

14 Ueda, *Ueda Shizuteru Shū* Vol. 9, 154.
15 Ueda, *Ueda Shizuteru Shū* Vol. 9, 155.
16 Ueda Shizuteru and John C. Marldo, "The Zen Buddhist experience of the truly beautiful," *The Eastern Buddhist* 22, no. 1 (1989): 2–3. The article was originally published in German: Shizuteru Ueda, "Die zen-buddhistische Erfahrung des Wahr-Schönen," in *Eranos Yearbook* 53, ed. Rudolf Ritsema (Frankfurt: Insel Verlag, 1984), 197–240.
17 Ueda, *Ueda Shizuteru Shū* Vol. 9, 155.
18 Ueda, *Ueda Shizuteru Shū* Vol. 9, 155.
19 Nishida, "*Junsuikeiken ni kansuru danshō*," 430.
20 Nishida, "*Nihon bunka no mondai*," 346.
21 Nishitani, *Religion and Nothingness*, 128.
22 Quoted in Ueda and Maraldo, "Zen Buddhist experience," 4.
23 Ueda and Maraldo, "Zen Buddhist experience," 10–11.
24 Martin Heidegger, *The Principle of Reason*, trans. Reginald Lilly (Bloomington and Indianapolis: Indiana University Press, 1991), 113.
25 Ueda and Maraldo, "Zen Buddhist experience," 15.
26 Erol Čopelj and Yuko Ishihara, "The transition: from being-in-the-world to nature-naturing," in *The Dialectic of Absolute Nothingness: The Legacy of German Philosophy in the Kyoto School*, ed. Gregory S. Moss and Takeshi Morisato (Ithaca: Cornell University Press, forthcoming).
27 Erol Čopelj, "Mindfulness: the feeling of being tuned-in, and related phenomena: phenomenological reflections of a Buddhist practitioner," PhD dissertation (Monash University /University of Warwick, 2019).
28 Erol Čopelj, *Phenomenological Reflections on Mindfulness in the Buddhist Tradition* (Abingdon: Routledge, 2022).
29 Ueda, *Ueda Shizuteru Shū* Vol. 9, 155.
30 Tetsurō Watsuji, *Ningen no gaku toshite no rinrigaku* [Ethics as a Study of Human Beings] (Tokyo: Iwanami Shoten, 2007), 18–38.
31 This point is crucially connected to many comments we made in Chapter 5.
32 Shizuteru Ueda, *Ueda Shizuteru Shū Vol. 4* (*Zen: Kongenteki ningen* [Zen: Fundamental Human Being]) (Tokyo: Iwanami Shoten, 2001), 296–302.
33 Mumon Yamada, *Rinzairoku* (Kyoto: The Institute for Zen Studies, 1984), 18.

Bibliography

Bernet, Rudolf. "Phenomenological and aesthetic *epoché*: painting the invisible things themselves." In *The Oxford Handbook of Contemporary Phenomenology*, edited by Dan Zahavi. Oxford: Oxford University Press, 2012, 564–582.

Chilcott, Tim. "Matsuo Bashō: *Oku no Hosomichi*, The Narrow Road to the Deep North." *Tim Chilcott Literary Translations*, 2004, 3. http://www.tclt.org.uk/basho/Oku_2011.pdf.

Čopelj, Erol. "Mindfulness: the feeling of being tuned-in, and related phenomena: phenomenological reflections of a Buddhist practitioner." PhD dissertation. Monash University /University of Warwick, 2019.

Čopelj, Erol. *Phenomenological Reflections on Mindfulness in the Buddhist Tradition*. Abingdon: Routledge, 2022.

Čopelj, Erol and Yuko Ishihara. "The transition: from being-in-the-world to nature-naturing." In *The Dialectic of Absolute Nothingness: The Legacy of German Philosophy in the Kyoto School,* edited by Gregory S. Moss and Takeshi Morisato. Ithaca: Cornell University Press, forthcoming.

Davis, Bret W. "Natural freedom: human/nature non-dualism in Japanese thought." In *The Oxford Handbook of World Philosophy*, edited by Jay Garfield and William Edelglass. New York: Oxford University Press, 2011, 334–347.

Dreyfus, Georges B. J. *Recognizing Reality: Dharmakirti's Philosophy and its Tibetan Interpretations*. Albany: SUNY Press, 1997.

Ebara, Taizō 穎原退蔵, ed. *Kyoraishō, Sanzōshi, Tabineron* 『去来抄・三冊子・旅寝論』. Tokyo: Iwanami Shoten, 1993.

Fink, Eugen. *Play as the Symbol of the World.* Translated by Ian Alexander Moore and Christopher Turner. Bloomington and Indianapolis: Indiana University Press, 2016.

Gadamer, Hans-Georg. *Truth and Method*. Translated by Joel Weinsheimer and Donald G. Marsh. London and New York: Continuum, 2004.

Gold, Jonathan C. "Vasubandhu." *The Stanford Encyclopedia of Philosophy* (Spring 2021 Edition), edited by Edward N. Zalta. https://plato.stanford.edu/archives/spr2021/entries/vasubandhu/.

Gopnik, Alison. "Could David Hume have known about Buddhism?: Charles François Dolu, the Royal College of La Flèche, and the Global Jesuit Intellectual Network." *Hume Studies* 35, Numbers 1 and 2 (2009): 5–28.

Heidegger, Martin. *The Principle of Reason*. Translated by Reginald Lilly. Bloomington and Indianapolis: Indiana University Press, 1991.

Husserl, Edmund. *Ideas Pertaining to a Pure Phenomenology and to a Phenomenological Philosophy: First Book*. Translated by Fred Kersten. The Hague: Martinus Nijhoff, 1983.

Husserl, Edmund. "Beilage IX: Persönliche Aufzeichnungen vom 25.9.1905, 4.11.1907 und 6.3.1908." In *Einleitung in die Logik und Erkenntnistheorie Vorlesungen 1906/07 Husserliana* 24. Den Haag: Nijhoff, 1984, 442–449.

Husserl, Edmund. *The Crisis of European Sciences and Transcendental Phenomenology: An Introduction to Phenomenological Philosophy*. Translated by David Carr. Evanston: Northwestern University, 1988.

Husserl, Edmund. *On the Phenomenology of the Consciousness of Internal Time (1893–1917)*. Edited and translated by J. B. Brough. Dordrecht: Kluwer, 1991.

Ishihara, Yuko 石原悠子. "Transcendental philosophy and its transformations: Heidegger and Nishida's critical engagements with transcendental philosophy in the late 1920s." PhD dissertation. University of Copenhagen, 2016.

Ishihara, Yuko 石原悠子. "Nishida Kitarō's awakened realism: going radically transcendental." *Metodo: International Studies in Phenomenology and Philosophy*, Special Issue 1.3: On the Transcendental (2019): 57–84. https://doi.org/10.19079/metodo.s1.3.57.

Nishida and Ueda on philosophical reflection." In *Tetsugaku Companion to Ueda Shizuteru: Language, Experience, and Zen* (Series: *Tetsugaku Companions to Japanese Philosophy*), ed. Raquel Bouso et al. (Cham: Springer, 2022).

Lenkowski, William J. "What is Husserl's epoché? The problem of the beginning of philosophy in a Husserlian context." *Man and World* 11 (1978): 299–323.

Lusthaus, Dan. *Buddhist Phenomenology: A Philosophical Investigation of Yogacara Buddhism and the Ch'eng Wei-shih Lun*. New York: Routledge, 2003.

MacAvoy, Leslie. "Distanciation and *epoché*: the influence of Husserl on Ricoeur's hermeneutics." In *Hermeneutics and Phenomenology in Paul Ricoeur: Between Text and Phenomenon*, edited by Scott Davidson and Marc-Antoine Vallée. Dordrecht: Springer, 2016, 13–30.

Nishida, Kitarō 西田幾多郎. "*Nihon bunka no mondai*" 「日本文化の問題」 [The problems of Japanese culture]. In *Nishida Kitarō Zenshū* 西田幾多郎全集 Vol. 12, edited by Yoshishige Abe et al. Tokyo: Iwanami Shoten, 1979, 275–383.

Nishida, Kitarō 西田幾多郎. "*Junsuikeiken ni kansuru danshō*" 純粋経験に関する断章 [Fragmentary notes on pure experience]. In *Nishida Kitarō Zenshū* 西田幾多郎全集 Vol. 16 (*Shoki sōkō* 初期草稿 [*Early Writings*]), edited by Yoshishige Abe et al. Tokyo: Iwanami Shoten, 1980, 267–572.

Nishida, Kitarō 西田幾多郎. *An Inquiry into the Good*. Translated by Masao Abe and Christopher Ives. New Haven and London: Yale University Press, 1990.

Nishida Kitarō Ibokushū Editorial Board 西田幾多郎遺墨集編集委員会, ed. *Nishida Kitarō Ibokushū* 西田幾多郎遺墨集. Kyoto: Tōeisha, 1977.

Nishitani, Keiji 西谷啓治. *Religion and Nothingness*. Translated by Jan van Bragt. Berkeley: University of California Press, 1982.

Nishitani, Keiji 西谷啓治. "*Bashō ni tsuite*" 「芭蕉について」 [On Bashō]. In *Shūkyo to Hishūkyo no aida* 『宗教と非宗教の間』 [*Between Religion and Non-religion*], edited by Shizuteru Ueda. Tokyo: Iwanami Shoten, 2001, 130–170.

Nishitani, Keiji 西谷啓治. "*Gyō to iu koto*" 「行ということ」 [To practice]. In *Shūkyo to Hishūkyo no aida* 『宗教と非宗教の間』 [*Between Religion and Non-religion*], edited by Shizuteru Ueda. Tokyo: Iwanami Shoten, 2001, 95–113.

Ricoeur, Paul. "Appropriation". In *Hermeneutics and the Human Sciences: Essays on Language, Action and Interpretation*, edited and translated by John B. Thompson. Cambridge: Cambridge University Press, 1981, 144–156.

Ricoeur, Paul. "Phenomenology and hermeneutics". In *Hermeneutics and the Human Sciences: Essays on Language, Action and Interpretation*, edited and translated by John B. Thompson. Cambridge: Cambridge University Press, 1981, 61–90.

Sarao, Karam Tej Singh. "Vasubandhu." *The Internet Encyclopedia of Philosophy*, September 25, 2022. https://iep.utm.edu/vasubandhu/.

Sartre, Jean-Paul. *The Imaginary: A Phenomenological Psychology of the Imagination*. Translated by Jonathan Webber. London and New York: Routledge, 2004.

Suzuki, Daisetsu T. 鈴木大拙. *Manual of Zen Buddhism*. New York: Grove Publishing, 1994.

Takeuchi, Seiichi 竹内整一. *"Onozukara" to "Mizukara": Nihon shisō: no kisō* 『「おのずから」と「みずから」—日本思想の基層』 [*"Onozukara" and "Mizukara": The Basis of Japanese Thought*]. Tokyo: Shunjyūsha, 2004.

Takeuchi, Seiichi 竹内整一. *Nihonjin wa naze "sayonara" to wakareru noka* 『日本人はなぜ「さようなら」と別れるのか』 [*Why Japanese People Say "Sayonara"*] (Chikuma Shinsho Series). Tokyo: Chikuma Shobō, 2009.

Tulku, Tarthang. *Time, Space & Knowledge: A New Vision of Reality*. Berkeley: Dharma Publishing, 1977.

Ueda, Shizuteru 上田閑照. "Die zen-buddhistische Erfahrung des Wahr-Schönen." In *Eranos Yearbook* 53, edited by Rudolf Ritsema. Frankfurt: Insel Verlag, 1984, 197–240.

Ueda, Shizuteru 上田閑照. *Nishida Kitarō o yomu* 『西田幾多郎を読む』 [*Reading Nishida Kitarō*]. Tokyo: Iwanami Shoten, 1991.

Ueda, Shizuteru 上田閑照. *Ueda Shizuteru Shū Vol. 4. Zen: Kongenteki ningen*『禅—根源的人間』 [*Zen: Fundamental Human Being*]). Tokyo: Iwanami Shoten, 2001.

Ueda, Shizuteru 上田閑照. *Ueda Shizuteru Shū* 上田閑照集 *Vol. 2: Keiken to jikaku* 『経験と自覚』. Tokyo: Iwanami Shoten, 2002.

Ueda, Shizuteru 上田閑照. *Ueda Shizuteru Shū* 上田閑照集 *Vol. 9* (*Kokū/Sekai* 『虚空/世界』 [*Open Expanse/World*]). Tokyo: Iwanami Shoten, 2002.

Ueda, Shizuteru 上田閑照. *Ueda Shizuteru Shū* 上田閑照集 *Vol. 6* (*Dōtei "Jūgyūzu" o ayumu* 『道程「十牛図」を歩む』 [*Walking the Passage "Ten Oxherding Pictures"*]). Tokyo: Iwanami Shoten, 2003.

Ueda, Shizuteru 上田閑照 and John C. Maraldo. "The Zen Buddhist experience of the truly beautiful." *The Eastern Buddhist* 22, number 1 (1989): 1–36.

Velez, Abraham. "Buddha (c. 500s B.C.E)." *The Internet Encyclopedia of Philosophy*, September 25, 2022. https://iep.utm.edu/buddha/.

Vilhauer, Monica. *Gadamer's Ethics of Play: Hermeneutics and the Other*. Plymouth: Lexington Books, 2010.
Watsuji, Tetsurō 和辻哲郎. *Ningen no gaku toshite no rinrigaku* 『人間の学としての倫理学』 [*Ethics as a Study of Human Beings*]. Tokyo: Iwanami Shoten, 2007.
Westerhoff, Jan Christoph. "Nāgārjuna." *The Stanford Encyclopedia of Philosophy* (Summer 2022 Edition), edited by Edward N. Zalta. https://plato.stanford.edu/archives/sum2022/entries/nagarjuna/.
Yamada, Mumon 山田無文. *Rinzairoku* 臨済録. Kyoto: The Institute for Zen Studies, 1984.
Zahavi, Dan. "Applied phenomenology: why it is safe to ignore the epoché." *Continental Philosophy Review* 54 (2021): 259–273. https://doi.org/10.1007/s11007-019-09463-y.

INDEX